APRIL 18, 2018
OCCURED BEFORE
MAY 8, 2018

APRIL 18, 2018 OCCURED BEFORE MAY 8, 2018

Crimen Omnia Ex Se Nata Vitiat
A Legal Description of Judicial Corruption in Cook County

(Exhibits and videos are on the website www.frankjbarrett.com)

Frank Barrett

ISBN: 979-8-3494-9899-2 (Paperback)
ISBN: 979-8-3494-9900-5 (eBook)

Printed in the United States of America

APRIL 18, 2018 OCCURRED BEFORE MAY 8, 2018

CRIMEN OMNIA EX SE NATA VITIA

A LEGAL DESCRIPTION OF JUDICIAL CORRUPTION IN COOK COUNTY,

LOT1

EXHIBIT 1 at LOT 1.com and **"multiple times"** in the record of an entirely vitiated 18 CH 13221 is the actual genuine material criminal April 18, 2018 **"demand letter"** as admitted and verified by a Robert Wilson as an authorized Vice President of Byline Bank and as prepared by a Scott Kenig as the then actual Attorney for Byline Bank.

As evidenced herein, first Kenig and then Cook County Judge Edward Robles; and then Appellate Court Judges Navarro and Mitchell and Mikva have criminally conspired for seven years with identical criminal frauds upon the court to fraudulently deny that actual genuine material criminal April 18, 2018 **"demand letter"** as prepared by Kenig ever existed; to criminally deny that it was Byline Bank that had caused the criminal fraudulently foreclosure of Frank and Darlene Barretts' actual continuous one Property; for Byline to criminally seize the Barretts' actual continuous one Property for vastly below its then fair market value of $630,000.00:

APRIL 18, 2018 OCCURRED BEFORE MAY 8, 2018

SEVEN YEARS

EXHIBIT 2 at LOT 1.com and **"multiple times"** in the record of that entirely vitiated 18 CH 13221 is the actual genuine material Plat of Survey for the Barretts' actual continuous one Property with the actual genuine material legal description for the Barretts' actual continuous one Property:

The Barretts' actual totally physically attached and united **"four-sided"** 1600-1606 Westchester Boulevard has always been totally located on that 100= foot= wide East of that Vacated Alley:

Lot 1 in George f. Nixon and Company's Central Addition to Westchester, being a Subdivision ....

As evidenced **"multiple times"** in the record of that entirely vitiated 18 CH 13221 by Kenig, that 100 foot wide East of that Vacated Alley Lot 1 is in the very actual genuine material . Legal Descriptions of the Barretts' actual Mortgages with Byline that Byline was causing the criminal fraudulent foreclosure of.

As evidenced, first that same Kenig and those same Judges Robles and then Navarro and Mitchell and Mikva still fraudulently denied the Barretts' actual 100-foot-wide East of that Vacated Alley Lot 1 ever existed with identical criminally fabricated physically impossible frauds upon the court to fraudulently deny that it was Byline that had caused the criminal fraudulent foreclosure of the Barretts' actual continuous one Property.

The Barretts' actual detached residential garage has always been located on continuous Lot 3 and that part of continuous Lot 5.

SEE: 1600-1606 Westchester Boulevard

EXHIBIT 3 at LOT 1.com is the actual genuine material **"as built"** blueprint of the Barretts' actual **"four sided"** 1600-1606 as on file with the Westchester Fire Department.

The Barretts' actual single story Westchester Medical Center, 1600, has always been totally physically attached and united by an interior foundation wall; a common wall/masonry fire barrier and joined by a custom built interior door to the Barretts' personal residence,1606, as an inseparable and permanently bound **"four-sided"** mixed-use building contained under one roof as:

1600-1606 is ONE mixed-use building
SEE: 1600-1606 Westchester Boulevard

As evidenced, first that same Kenig and then those same Judges Robles and Navarro and Mitchell and Mikva committed identical criminal fraudulently fabricated physically impossible absurd frauds upon the court to fraudulently deny that the Barretts' actual 100 foot wide East of that Vacated Alley Lot 1 ever existed to then fraudulently deny the Barretts' actual **"four-sided"** totally attached and united 1600-1606 ever existed; to fraudulently deny that it was Byline that had caused the criminal fraudulent foreclosure of the Barretts' actual continuous one Property:

"four-sided"

Only the Cook County Assessor is authorized by statute, 35 ILCS 200/9-150, to classify real property in Cook County for real estate taxation purposes and must do so according to the actual use of property.

A PIN (Property Index Number) is a numerical code for the legal description of a piece of land as it has been defined for real estate taxation purposes. A PIN points to a parcel's location on the Cook County tax maps.

The eighth nineth and tenth digit of every PIN is always a parcel number: **ALWAYS.**

Pursuant to the Cook County Assessor Definition of Codes for Real Property:

Class 201: residential garage

Class 203: one-story residence, any age, 1,000 to 1,800 square feet

Class 2-12: mixed=use commercial/residential building with apartment and commercial units totaling 6 units or less with square footage of less than 20,000 square feet

Class 517: single-story commercial building

Pursuant to Cook County Ordinance for Assessment Level:

Class 201: 10% of estimated market value

Class 203: 10% of estimated market value

Class 2-12: 10% of estimated market value

Class 517: 25% of estimated market value

Cook County Classification 2-12 property tax bills are always 60% less than Cook County Classification 517 property tax bills:

ALWAYS

EXHIBIT 4 at LOT 1.com is the actual genuine material Sidwell Cook County property tax map for the Barretts' actual continuous one Property.

As corroborated by the actual Plat of Survey of the Barretts' actual continuous one Property, the Barretts' actual **"four-sided"** totally attached and united 1600-1606 has always been located entirely on that 100-foot-wide Lot 1 East of that Vacated Alley.

As evidenced, first that same Kenig and then those same Robles and then Navarro and Mitchell and Mikva fraudulently deny that the Barretts' actual100- foot- wide Lot 1 East of that Vacated Alley ever existed; to criminally deny the Barretts' actual **"four-sided"** totally attached and united 1600-1606 ever existed; to criminally deny that it was Byline that had caused the criminal fraudulent foreclosure of the Barretts' actual continuous one Property.

The Barretts' actual detached residential garage has always been located on that continuous Lot 3 and that continuous part of Lot 5.

For real estate taxation purposes, the Barretts' actual single story totally attached and united Westchester Medical Center, 1600, is located on that continuous North 66.77· foot wide of Lot 1: Property Index Number 15-21-301-206-0000 (PIN 206).

For real estate taxation purposes, the Barretts' actual single=story totally attached and united personal residence, 1606, is located on that continuous South 34.23-foot-wide of Lot 1:Property Index Number 15-21=301-207-0000 (PIN 207).

For real estate taxation purposes, the Barretts' actual detached residential garage is located on continuous Property Index Number 15-21-301-209-0000 (PIN 209).

EXHIBIT 5 at LOT 1.com is the Cook County Treasurer 2016 Second Installment Property Tax Bill for PIN 206, which use is the Barrett's actual totally attached and united Westchester Medical Center, 1600:

The 2016 classification was Class 517 to be assessed at 25% of estimated market value; the 2016 Assessed Value was $63,025; and the 2016 Total Tax was $18,380.95.

As admitted herein by the Cook County Assessor on February 13, 2018:

THE CLASS WAS INCORRECT BASED UPON USE OF THE PROPERTY

The Assessor's **"PROPERTY"** is the continuous North 66.77 feet of Lot 1 East of that Vacated Alley.

EXHIBIT 6 at LOT 1.com is the Cook County Treasurer 2016 Second Installment Property Tax Bill for continuous PIN 207, which use is the Barretts' totally attached and united personal residence, 1606.

The 2016 classification was Class 203 to be assessed at 10% of estimated market value; the 2016 Assessed Value was $15,028; and the 2016 Total Tax was $2,921.65

As admitted herein by the Cook County Assessor on February 13, 2018:

THE CLASS WAS INCORRECT BASED ON USE OF THE PROPERTY

The Assessor's **"PROPERTY"** is the continuous South 34.23 feet of Lot 1East of that Vacated Alley.

As evidenced herein, first Kenig and then Robles and then Navarro and Mitchell and Mikva fraudulent deny the Barretts' actual 100-foot-wide Lot 1 East of that Vacated Alley ever existed to fraudulently deny that the Barretts actual **"four-sided"** totally attached and united 1600-1606 ever existed to fraudulently deny that it was Byline that caused the criminal fraudulent foreclosure of the Barretts' actual continuous one Property.

In July of 2017 the Barretts engaged the services of Raila & Associates, a real estate tax attorney association, to correctly reclassify PIN 206, which actual use is the Barretts' totally attached and united Westchester Medical Center, 1600, from Class 517, being assessed at 25% of market value, to Class 2-1 to be assessed at 10% of market value, and to have continuous PIN 207, which actual use is the Barretts' totally attached and united personal residence, 1606, also correctly reclassified from Class 203, being assessed at 10% of market value, to Class 2-12 to still be assessed at 10% of market value, based upon the actual use of 100-foot- wide Lot 1 East of that Vacated Alley.

EXHIBIT 7 at LOT 1.com is the Cook County Assessor standard BUILDING RECORD RESIDENTIAL for PIN 207, which use is the Barretts' actual totally attached and united personal residence, 1606, with a diagram of the Barretts' actual **"four-sided"** totally attached and united 1600-1606:

Per intemal
inspection,
there is a door
joining the residential
unit to com unit
Q-UP 2-12 w/4068#

1600-1606 is ONE mixed-use building
SEE: 1600-1606 Westchester Boulevard

PRORATION BREAKDOWN
70 % TO PAR 206
30 % TO PAR 207
%TO PAR

It is not uncommon in Cook County for a building to be on two or more continuous parcels for property taxation purposes. The Cook County Assessor standard BUILDING RECORD RESIDENTIAL provided for such.

The Barretts' 6 car detached garage is located on that continuous PIN 209.

Doc 113229 is the actual 2017 Assessment Appeal Number for the Barretts' PIN 206 and continuous PIN 207.

As evidenced, first that same Kenig and then those same Robles and then Navarro and Mitchell and Mikva fraudulently deny that the Cook County Assessor Inspector ever correctly determined for real estate property taxation purposes:

Q-UP 2-12 w/4068#

To fraudulently deny that it was Byline that had caused the criminal fraudulent foreclosure of the Barretts' actual continuous one Property.

Pursuant to the Barretts' actual 2017 Assessment Appeal Number 011329 for PIN 206 and continuous PIN 207 and that internal inspection of the Barretts' actual **"four sided"** 1600- 1606 by that Cook County Assessor Inspector, EXHIBIT 8 at LOT 1.com is the October 9, 2017 letter from the Cook County Assessor to Raila:

2017 Assessment Appeal
Township: PROVISO
Appeal Number: 0113329
Property Index Number(s)
15-21-301-206-0000
15-21-301-207-0000

As evidenced, Kenig forever fraudulently denies that the Barretts' actual 2017 Appeal Number 0113329 for PIN 206 and continuous PIN 207 ever existed and was ever filed with the Cook County Assessor to forever fraudulently deny that it was Byline that had caused the criminal fraudulent foreclosure of the Barretts' actual continuous one Property.

I am pleased to inform you that om appeals department has reviewed your appeal and determined that the assessed valuation of your property should be reduced. Your new assessed value is indicated below.

As evidenced, Kenig forever fraudulently denies that the Barretts' actual 2017 Assessment Appeal Number 0113329 for PIN 206 and continuous PIN 207 was ever already granted by the Cook County Assessor on that October 9, 2017 to forever fraudulently deny that it was Byline that had caused the criminal fraudulent foreclosure of the Barretts' actual continuous one Property.

This is a result of a change in classification.

As evidenced, Kenig forever fraudulently denies there was ever a change in classifications for PIN 206 and continuous PIN 207 to forever fraudulently deny that it was Byline that had caused the criminal fraudulent foreclosure of the Barretts' actual continuous one Property.

This reduction will be reflected on the second installment your 2017 real estate tax bill payable in 2018.

The Assessor's actual **"reduction"** is the **"reduction"** of the assessed values for PIN 206 and continuous PIN 207, and not a **"reduction"** in taxes, to be reflected on the Cook County Assessor Second Installment Property Tax Bills for PIN 206 and continuous PIN 207.

ORIGINAL CLASS	PROPERTY INDEX NUMBER	2016 PRIOR ASSESSED VALUE	PROPOSED 2017 ASSESSED VALUE	2017 CURRENT AV
517	**15-21-301-206-0000**	**63,025**	**79,753**	**29,019**
503	**15-21-301-207-0000**	**15,020**	**18,031**	**12,648**

As evidenced, Kenig forever fraudulently denies that on October 9, 2017 that the 2017 CURRENT AV of PIN 206 was ever $29,019 to forever fraudulently deny that it was Byline that had caused the criminal fraudulent foreclosure of the Barretts' actual continuous one property.

The Assessor's decision on the Barretts' 2017 Assessment Appeal for PIN 206 and continuous PIN 207 would not become Final on its Website until PROVISO Township was totally CERTIFIED by the Assessor.

PIN 206, which actual use is the Barretts' single story totally attached and united Westchester Medical Center, 1600, and PIN 209, which actual use is the Barretts' detached residential garage, were the collateral for Loan #11147585 which was to expire in September of 2018.

PIN 207, which actual use is the Barretts' single story totally attached and united personal residence, 1606, was the collateral for Loan #11147245 which was also to expire in September of 2018.

EXHIBIT 9 at LOT 1 is Byline's ANNUAL ESCROW DISCLOSURE STATEMENT for Loan #11147585 as dated October 31, 2017 with PIN 206 still incorrectly classified as Class 517 to be assessed at 25% of market value and a then 2016 Assessed Value of $63,025.

YOUR NEW PAYMENT INFORMATION

PRINC & INT	$1,455.55
ESCROW	1,671.45
DATE 1/16/18	$3,271.00

PROJECTED PAYMENTS FROM YOUR ESCROW THIS CYCLE

TAXES-COOK CTY 1ST INST 10669.13

Pursuant to statute, the Barretts had to pay 55% of the then 2016 property taxes for PIN 206 and PIN 209 due on March 1, 2018.

TAXES-COOKCTY-2ND INST 8981.32

On that October 31, 2017 the PROJECTED 2nd Installment property tax bill for PIN 206 and PIN 209 was that $8,981.32

19659.45

On that October 31, 2017 the PROJECTED 2017 Total Tax for PIN 206 and PIN 209 was that $19,659.45.

MONTH	PAYMENTS TO ESCROW	PAYMENTS FROM ESCROW DESCRIPTION	ESCROW BALANCE
2/18	1637		4068.70

As admitted and verified by Kenig on October 23, 2018 with a **"screen shot"** of Byline's actual computer generated records for Loan #11147585, after the Barretts' February 16, 2018 payment of $3,271.00 to Byline for Loan #1147585 no further payment of any amount of **"ESCROW"** was ever **"due and owing"** nor ever **"required"** of the Barretts by Byline for Loan #11147585 under the actual provisions of Loan #11147585.

7/18	**10618.85**
8/18	**3275.08 RLP**

(RLP) REQUIRED LOW POINT BALANCE

As admitted and verified by Kenig on October 23, 2018 the Barretts always maintained Byline's REQUIRED LOW POINT BALANCE of that $3,275.08.

As such, Byline could never, and never did, issue any **"demand letter"** for any **"Escrow"** of any amount nor at any time for Loan #11147585 and Byline could never, and never did, **"declare"** any **"Event of Default"** of any nature nor at any time in the Barretts' actual real estate property tax escrow account for Loan #11147585 under the actual provisions of Loan #11147585; exactly because there never was any "Event of Default" of any nature nor at any time in the Barretts' actual real estate property tax escrow account for Loan #11147585.

EXHIBIT 10 at LOT 1.com on its Website as of November 18, 2017 is the Assessor's Appeal History for PIN 206, which use is the Barretts' actual totally physically attached and united Westchester Medical Center, 1600.

Status:
Status Date:
Prior Value: 63,025
Current Value: 29,019
Result: Assessed Value Adjusted. This is a result of a change in classification.

As evidenced, first Kenig and then Robles and then Navarro and Mitchell and Mikva fraudulently deny the Assessed Value of PIN 206 was ever adjusted to $29,019 and fraudulently deny there was ever a change in the classification of PIN 206 to fraudulently deny that it was Byline that had caused the criminal fraudulent foreclosure of the Barretts' actual continuous one Property.

As of that November 18, 2017 on the Assessor's Website, PIN 206 was correctly reclassified from Class 517 being assessed at 25% of market value to Class 2-12 being assessed at 10% of market value and the 2016 Final Assessed Value $63,025 of PIN 206 was adjusted to a 2017 Final Assessed Value of $29,019.

As evidenced, first Kenig and then Robles and then Navarro and Mitchell and Mikva fraudulently deny that PIN 206 could ever have been Class 2-12 to be assessed at 10% of market value but could only always Kenig's fraudulently fabricated **"misclassification"** of Class 517 to be assessed at 25% of market value to fraudulently deny that it was Byline that had caused the criminal fraudulent foreclosure of the Barretts' actual continuous one Property.

EXHIBIT 11 at LOT 1.com on its Website as of November 18, 2017 is the Assessor's Appeal History for continuous PIN 207, which actual use is the Barretts' actual totally physically attached and united personal residence, 1606:

Status:
Status Date:
Prior Value: 15,0211
Current Value: 12,846
Result: Assessed Value Adjusted. This is a result of a change in classification.

As evidenced first Kenig and then Robles and then Navarro and Mitchell and Mikva fraudulently deny the Assessed Value of PIN 207 was ever adjusted and there was ever a change in classification for continuous PIN 207 to fraudulently deny that it was Byline that had caused the criminal fraudulent foreclosure of the Barretts' actual continuous one Property.

As of that November 18, 2017 on the Assessor's Website PIN 207 was correctly reclassified from Class 203 to Class 2-12.

As evidenced first Kenig and then Navarro and Mitchell and Mikva fraudulently denied that continuous PIN 207 could ever have been Class 2-12 but was always Class 203 to fraudulently deny that it was Byline that had caused the criminal fraudulent foreclosure of the Barretts' actual continuous one Property.

The changes in classifications to Class 2-12 for PIN 206 and continuous PIN 207 would be reflected on the 1st installment of property tax bills for PIN 206 and continuous PIN 207 due on March 1, 2018.

Upon those changes in classifications to Class 2-12 for PIN 206 and continuous PIN 207 by the Assessor on November 18, 2017, Raila filed six Certificates of Error for PIN 206 and continuous PIN 207 for the years 2014, 2015 and 2016 for refunds by the Cook County Treasurer.

On that November 18, 2017 pursuant to the records that existed of Byline and the Assessor and the Cook County Treasurer, the PROJECTED 2nd installment property tax bill for PIN 206, which actual use is the Barretts' totally physically attached and united Westchester Medical Center, 1600, due on August 1, 2018 was:

$0.00

And the PROJECTED 2nd installment property tax bill for PIN 209, which actual use is the Barretts' detached residential garage, due on August 1, 2018 was:

$571.24

On that November 18, 2017 the PROJECTED 2nd installment property tax bill for Loan #11147585 due on August 1, 2018 was that:

$571.24

EXHIBIT 12 at LOT 1.com is Frank Barretts' November 18, 2017 e=mail to Rosemarie Viramontes, a Byline Loan Officer:

HI ROSEMARIE:

AT THE COOK COUNTY ASSESSOR WEBSITE APPEAL HISTORT/CHECK STATUS

15-21-301-206-0000 FOR THE OFFICE

2016 2017
FINAL FINAL
63,025 29,019
15-21-301-207-0000 FOR OUR HOME
2016 2017
FINAL FINAL
15,020 12,848

As evidenced, Kenig forever fraudulently denied that Frank Barrett had ever **"advised"** Byline that on November 18, 2017 on its Website at Appeal History History/Check Status that the Assessor had already adjusted the 2016 Final Assessed Value of $63,025 for PIN 206 to a 2017 Final Assessed Value of $29,019 for PIN 206 to forever fraudulently deny that it was Byline that had caused the criminal fraudulent foreclosure of the Barretts' actual continuous one Property.

BOTH OF MY REAL ESTATE TAX BILLS WiIl GO DOWN SIGNIFICANT

Just as significantly, the fair market value of the Barretts' actual continuous one Property would increase as a result of the significant reduction on the 2017 Assessed Value of PIN 206 to that Final $29,019.

That, of course, is exactly why Byline caused the criminal fraudulent foreclosure of the Barretts' actual continuous one Property.

Even though under the actual provisions of Loan #11147585 as admitted by Kenig on October 23, 2018 that after the Barretts' February 16, 2018 payment of $3,271.00 to Byline that no further **"Escrow"** payments of any amount were ever **"due and owing"** nor ever **"required"** of the Barretts by Byline, Frank Barrett still offered to pay $500 per month to Byline in hopes of retaining the vastly below market interest rate of 4% which could then be renegotiated in October of 2018.

Pursuant to the November 21, 2017 e-mail of Byline Loan Officer Mark Hansen to Frank Barrett:

Thank you, Mr. Barrett

EXHIBIT 13 at LOT 1.com is the November 28, 2017 e-mail of Byline Loan Officer Mark Hansen to Frank Barrett:

Mr. Barrett, I have asked our escrow department to manually re-cut the escrow analysis based on the information you have provided. I will provide you with an update as soon as that is completed.

That **"information you provided"** on the Cook County Assessor Website at Appeal History Check Status **"verified"** to Byline that the 2nd property tax installment for Loan #11147585 would be significantly less than the 2nd installment property tax bill for Loan #11147585 as PROJECTED by Byline on October 31, 2017 exactly because of the significant reduction in the 2017 Assessed Value of $29,019 by the Assessor on its Website as of November 18, 2017.

As evidenced, Kenig forever fraudulently denies that "information" ever existed and was ever "provided" to Byline to forever fraudulently deny that it was Byline that had caused the criminal fraudulent foreclosure of the Barretts' actual one Property.

EXHIBIT 14 at LOT 1.com is the December 7, 2017 e-mail from Hansen to Frank Barrett:

Mr. Barret, they are asking for a copy of the letter you received from the County relative to the reduction in taxes via your appeal. Please either scan it to me or fax it to 312/5460-3195.

That **"letter you received from the County"** was the October 9, 2017 letter from the Assessor granting the Barretts' actual 2017 Assessment Appeal Number 0113329 for PIN 206 and continuous PIN 207.

That letter **"verified"** to Byline that the Barretts' actual 2017 Assessment Appeal Number 0113329 for PIN 206 and continuous PIN 207 did exist; was filed with the Assessor; was already granted by the Assessor on that October 9, 2017; and that the 2nd installment property tax bill for Loan #11147585 due on August 1, 2018 would be significantly less than the 2nd installment property tax for Loan #11147585 as PROJECTED by Byline on October 31, 2017 due to the significant reduction in the 2017 Assessed Value on PIN 206 to $29,019.

As evidenced, Kenig forever fraudulently denies the Barretts' actual 2017 Assessment Appeal Number 0113329 for PIN 206 and continuous PIN 207 ever existed; was ever filed with the Assessor; and was ever granted by the Assessor; to fraudulently deny that the 2017 CURRENT Value of PIN 206 was ever $29,019: to fraudulently deny that it was Byline that had caused the criminal fraudulent foreclosure of the Barretts' actual continuous one Property.

EXHIBIT 15 at LOT 1.com is Hansen's January 4, 2018 e-mail to Frank Barrett wherein Byline refused the Barretts' request to have the monthly escrow payments for Loan #11147585 be reduced to $500.00 per month based upon the significant reduction in the 2017 Assessed Value of PIN 206 by the Cook County Assessor to $29,019.

On that January 4, 2018 the PROJECTED 2nd installment property tax bill for Loan #11147585 due on August 1, 2018 was $571.24

As admitted by Kenig on October 23, 2018 under the actual provisions of Loan #11147585 after the Barretts' February 16, 2018 payment of $3,271.00 to Byline that no further **"Escrow"** payment of any amount for Loan #11147585 was ever **"due and owing"** nor ever **"required"** of the Barretts by Byline.

Despite those actual provisions of Loan #11147585, Byline was still demanding that on July 16, 2018 that $10,618.08 of the Barretts' money be on Byline's balance sheet to pay that 2nd real estate property tax bill of that $571.24 for Loan #11147585; one month before Loan #11147585 was due to expire.

On that January 4, 2018 it was already glaringly obvious to the Barretts that Byline had no intention whatsoever of renewing the Barretts' Loans with Byline and that Byline was already planning the foreclosure of the Barretts' Loans with Byline at the time of renewal in September of 2018.

On January 16, 2018 the Barretts paid Byline $3,271.00 for Loan #11147585 to **"properly fund"** the real property tax escrow account for Loan #11147585 to both maintain Byline's REQUIRED LOW POINT BALANCE and to also pay the statutory pt installment property tax bills for PIN 206 and PIN 209 due on March 1, 2018.

In the first week of February 2018 the State Equalizer was published. It increased by 0.02%

In that first week of February 2018 the now estimated 2nd installment property tax bill for Loan #11147585 was $620.02.

EXHIBIT 16 at LOT 1.com is the Cook County Treasurer 2017 First Installment Property Tax Bill for PIN 206:

Classification 2-12

On February 13, 2018 Byline paid that 1st installment property tax bill for PIN 206 of $10,109.52 as 55% of the then 2016 property tax for PIN 206 pursuant to statute.

EXHIBIT 17 at LOT 1.com is the Cook County Treasurer 2017 First Installment Property Tax Bill for continuous PIN 207:

Classification 2-12

On February 13, 2018 Byline paid that 2017 1st installment property tax bill for continuous PIN 207 of $1,606.85 as 55% of the 2016 property tax bill for continuous PIN 207 pursuant to statute.

Those two Classification 2-12 2017 Cook County Treasure Property Tax Bills for PIN 206 and continuous PIN 207 as paid by Byline on that February 13, 2018 **"verified"** to Byline that the Barretts' actual 2017 Assessment Appeal Number 0113329 for PIN 206 and continuous PIN 207 did exist; was filed with the Assessor; and had already been granted by the Assessor.

As evidenced, Kenig forever fraudulently denies the Barrett's 2017 Assessment Appeal Number 0113329 for PIN 206 and continuous PIN 2017 ever existed; was ever filed with the Assessor; and had already been granted by the Assessor as of that February 13, 2018 to forever fraudulently deny that it was Byline that had caused the criminal fraudulent foreclosure of the Barretts' actual continuous one Property.

EXHIBIT 18 at LOT 1.com is the Cook County Treasurer 2017 First Installment Property Tax Bill for PIN 209, which use is the Barretts' detached residential garage:

Classification 201

On February 13, 2018 Byline paid the 2017 1st installment property tax bill for PIN 209 of $698.23 as 55% of the 2016 property tax bill of PIN 209 pursuant to statute.

As verified by Frank Barrett with Byline's escrow department and then admitted and verified by Kenig on October 23, 2018, after Byline paid the 2017 1st installment statutory property tax bills for PIN 206 and PIN 209 on that February 13, 2018 the balance in the Barretts' property tax escrow account for Loan #11147585 was at least $3,348.00.

On February 16, 2018 the Barretts paid Byline $3,271.00 for Loan #11147585.

In doing so, the Barretts "properly funded" their actual real estate property tax escrow account for Loan #11147585 to both maintain Byline's REQUIRED LOW POINT BALANCE; and to also already prepay the actual 2nd installment real estate taxes for PIN 206 and PIN 209 due on August 1, 2018; and specifically overfunded $1,000.00 in **SURPLUS** to the property tax escrow account for Loan #11147585 to already prevent Byline from causing the foreclosure of the Barretts' actual continuous one Property.

SURPLUS

It is the **"universal right"** of every Mortgagor to **"overfond"** that Mortgagor's real estate property tax escrow account, particularly when a Bank is already planning the foreclosure of that Mortgagor's Property.

Then on October 23, 2018 Kenig will admit and verify that after the Barretts made that payment of that $3,271.00 to Byline for Loan #11147585 on February 16, 2018 that the balance in the Barretts' actual real estate escrow account for Loan #11147585 was at least $4,883.53; the Barretts' actual real estate property tax escrow account #11147585 was already both **"properly funded"**, with **SURPLUS**, to both maintain Byline's REQUIRED LOW POINT BALANCE and to also already pay the actual 2nd installment property tax bills for PIN 206 and PIN 209 due on August 1, 2018; and that no further payment of **"Escrow"** of any amount was **"due and owing"** nor **"required"** by the Barretts by Byline under the actual provisions of Loan #11147585:

SURPLUS

In the filed record of the entirely vitiated 18 CH 13221 are the six Certificates of Error as issued by the Cook County Assessor on February 13, 2018 for PIN 206 and continuous PIN 207 for the years 2014, 2015 and 2016 pursuant to the changes in classifications of PIN 206 and continuous PIN 207 to Class 2-12.

EXHIBIT 19 at LOT 1.com is the Certificate of Error for PIN 206 for 2016:

THE CLASS WAS INCORRECT BASED ON USE OF THE PROPERTY

The Assessor's **"PROPERTY"** is the continuous North 66.77 feet of 100 foot wide Lo1 East of that Vacated Alley:

RE: 15-21=301=206-0000
2016 CERTIFICATE OF ERROR NUMBER 004447952
CERTIFICATED ON: FEBRUARY 13, 2018
CERTIFICATE ASSESSED VALUE: 24,881
ORIGINAL TAX AMOUNT: 18,380.45
ADJUSTED TAX AMOUNT: 5,997.45

On October 31, 2017 PIN 206 was still Classification 517; the 2016 Assessed Value of PIN 206 was still $63,025; the 2016 TOTAL TAX for PIN 206 was still $18,380.45 and the 2016 **"aggregate"** tax bill for PIN 206 and PIN 209 was $$19,649.96.

On February 13, 2018 PIN 206 is Classification 2-12; the 2016 Assessed Value of PIN 206 is $24,881; the 2016 TOTAL TAX for PIN 206 is $5,997.45; and the 2016 **"aggregate"** tax bill for PIN 206 and PIN 209 is $7,266.956 due to the change in Classification 2=12 for PIN 206.

For the Barretts to receive those six refunds from the Cook County Treasurer of approximately $39,000.00 the Barretts had to prove to the Cook County Treasurer that the Barretts had paid the 2014; 2015; and 2016 property tax bills for PIN 206 and continuous PIN 207.

According, EXHIBIT 20 at LOT 1.com is Frank Barrett's February 27, 2018 e-mail to

HI MARK:

MY C OF ES FOR THE YEARS 2014, 2015 AND 2016 HAVE BEEN ACCEPTED BY THE COOK COUNTY TREASURER. FOR MYSELF TO OBTAIN THE SUBSTANTIAL REFUNDS I NEED PROOF OF PAYMENT THAT BYLINE BANK PAID THE REAL ESTATE TAXES FOR THOSE YEARS. PLEASE PROVIDE AT YOUR EARLIEST CONVENIENCE

Hansen provided those Classification 2-12 documents for PIN 206 and continuous PIN 207; Frank Barrett lodged those Classification 2-12 documents with the Cook County Treasurer; those refunds of approximately $39,000.00 were sent to Raila; and Raila forwarded those six refunds to the Barretts minus Raila's fees.

As evidenced, Kenig and then Robles and then Navarro and Mitchell and Mikva fraudulently deny those six Certificates of Error issued by the Assessor on February 13, 2018 for PIN 206 and continuous PIN 207 ever existed and deny the Barretts ever received those six refunds by fraudulently denying there was ever any change in the classifications of PIN 206 and continuous PIN 207 to Class 2-12 to fraudulently deny that it was Byline that had caused the criminal fraudulent foreclosure of the Barretts' actual one continuous Property.

EXHIBIT 21 at LOT 1.com is Byline's fraudulent Loan Payment Notice for Note #11147585 as dated March 1, 2018:

Principal Balance: **227,865.24**
Payment Due Date: **MAR 16, 2018**

Your Payment Consist of

Principal **746.72**
Interest **708.83**
Escrow **1,671.45**
Total Payment Due: **3,271.00**

As would be admitted and verified by Robert Wilson as an authorized Vice President of Byline on April 18, 2018 and by Kenig on October 23, 2018, under the actual provisions of Loan #11147585 all that was ever **"due and owing"** or **"required"** of the Barretts by Byline on March 16, 2018 was $1,455.55 for Principal & Interest exactly because PIN 206 was already Class 2-12 to be assessed at 10% of market value.

With PIN 206 still being Classification 517 to still be assessed at 25% of market value, on that March 16, 2018 that $1,671.45 Escrow payment would have been **"due and owing"** and **"required"** of the Barretts by Byline.

Despite on February 13, 2018 Byline having already paid the 2017 Classification 2-12 Cook County Treasurer First Installment Property Tax Bills for PIN 206 and continuous PIN 207 as the exact evidence to Byline that the Barretts' actual 2017 Assessment Appeal Number 0113329 for PIN 206 and continuous PIN 207 did exist; had been filed with the Assessor; and had already been granted by the Assessor, now on March 1, 2018 Byline was already denying that PIN 206 was ever Classification 2-12 to be assessed at 10% but was always Class 517 to be assessed at 25% of market value to cause the foreclosure of the Barretts' actual continuous one Property.

That fraudulently prepared by Byline March 1, 2018 loan Payment Notice for Note #11147585 was the exact inception of Byline's criminal conspiracy to de-fraud of causing the criminal fraudulent foreclosure of the Barretts' actual continuous one Property; for Byline to criminally seize the Barretts' actual continuous one Property for vastly below its then actual fair market value of $630,000.00.

As evidenced in the record of an entirety vitiated 18 CH 13221, on March 14, 2018 the Barretts started the process of refinancing their actual loans with Byline elsewhere prior to maturity.

On that March 14, 2018 the Barretts were willing to spend THOUSANDS OF DOLLARS in refinancing costs and refinance at a higher interest rates to already prevent Byline from causing the foreclosure of the Barretts actual continuous one Property.

Because of that fraudulent March 1, 2018 loan Payment Notice of Byline demanding that the Barretts were **"required"** to pay Byline $1,671.45 on March 16, 2018 for Escrow, EXHIBIT 22 at LOT 1.com is the Barretts' exact legal response as dated March 16, 2018 and before the Barretts made their March 16, 2018 monthly payment for loan #11147585:

HI MARK:

Today I am making my loan payment for Loan #11147585 with two checks marked P&I and Escrow.

The P&I check is for $1,455.55.

The Escrow check is for $400. I will continue to make Escrow payments of $400 per month.

The subject loan expires on September 16, 2018. As such, as of now there is no current reason to re-cut the escrow payments for 2019.

Pursuant to the official Cook County records sought and provided to the Credit Department, at present there is a SURPLUS in the real estate escrow account.

"Pursuant to the official Cook County records" as sought and provided to Byline and Byline's actual genuine computer records for loan #11147585, on that March 16, 2018 before the Barretts made those two payments to Byline the actual balance in the Barretts' real estate property tax escrow account for Loan #11147585 was at least $4,883.53; that escrow account was already both **"property funded"**, with **SURPLUS**, to both maintain Byline's REQUIRED LOW POINT BALANCE and to also already pay the actual 2017 2nd installment property taxes for Loan

#11147585 due on August 1, 2018; and no further **"Escrow"** payment of any amount was ever **"due owing"** nor ever **"required"** of the Barretts by Byline for Loan #11157585 under the actual provisions of Loan #11147585.

As such, for the April 16, 2018 payment for the subject loan there will be no shortage; no late payment and no late fees, only SURPLUS.

Then on October 23, 2018 Kenig will admit and verify that there was never any **"PAST DUE AMOUNT"** of any amount nor at any time for Loan #11147585; the Barretts made alt of their monthly payments to Byline as **"required"** under the actual provisions of Loan #11147585; the Barretts were never in any **"default"** of any nature under the actual provision of Loan #11147585' and that it was Byline that had caused the criminal fraudulent foreclosure of the Barretts' actual continuous one Property:

SURPLUS

EXHIBIT 23 at LOT 1.com is the Barretts' Check Number 809 as specifically marked **"#11141585 P&I"** in the amount of $1,455.55 dated March 16, 2018 and cashed by Byline on that March 16, 2018.

EXHIBIT 24 at LOT 1.com is the Barretts' Check Number 810 as specifically marked **"#11141585 ESCROW"** in the amount of $400.00 as dated March 16, 2018 and cashed by Byline on that March 16, 2018.

On that March 16, 2018 the Barretts again overfunded that $400.00 to the already **SURPLUS** in their property tax escrow account for Loan #11147585 to further prevent Byline from causing the fraudulent foreclosure of the Barretts' actual continuous one Property.

Then as admitted and verified by Kenig on October 23, 2018 with a **"screen shot"** of Byline's actual records for Loan #11147585, after the Barretts' payment of that $400.00 to **"Escrow"** for Loan #11147585 to Byline on that March 16, 2018 the balance in the Barretts' actual real estate property tax escrow account for Loan #11147585 was at least $5,283.53; that escrow account was already both **"properly funded"**, with **SURPLUS**, to both maintain Byline's REQUIRED LOW POINT BALANCE and to also already pay the actual 2nd installment real estate property tax for Loan #11147585 due on August 1, 2018; there was never any

PAST DUE AMOUNT of any amount for Loan #11147585; and no further **"Escrow"** payment of any amount was ever **"due and owing"** nor ever **"required"** of the Barretts by Byline for Loan #11147585 under the actual provisions of Loan #11147585 after the Barretts February 16, 2018 payment of $3,271.00 to Byline for Loan #11147585:

SURPLUS

EXHIBIT 25 at LOT 1.com is Byline's fraudulently fabricated **PAST DUE NOTICE** for Note #11147585 as dated March 26, 2018:

DEAR CUSTOMER

WE AGAIN CALL YOUR ATTENTION TO THE NOTE PAST DUE AS DESCRIBED HEREIN.

PRINCIPAL BALANCE	**226,409.69**
PAYMENT DUE DATE	**MAR 16,2018**
AMOUNT OF PAYMENT	**2,832.56**
PRINCIPAL	**746.72**
INTEREST	**308.83**
LATE CHARGES	**1,671.45**
TOTAL PAST DUE	**2,832.56**

MARCH 1, 2018 PRINCIPLE BALANCE	**227,865.24**
MARCH 26, 2018 PRINCIPLE BALANCE	**226,409.69**
	1,455.55

On that March 26, 2018 Byline fraudulently removed the Barretts' entire March 16, 2018 payment of $1,455.55 for **"P&I"** from the March 1, 2018 **"Your Payment Consists of"** to that fraudulent fabricated March 26, 2018 PRINCIPAL BALANCE of that $226,409.69 to fraudulently deny that Barretts' has made that March 16, 2018 payment of that $1,455.55 to **"P&I"** to fraudulently fabricate a **"default"** by the Barretts that never existed in their Principal & Interest account for Loan #11147585 to cause the criminal fraudulent foreclosure of the Barretts' actual continuous one Property.

Byline also fraudulently entered the Barretts' entire March 16, 2018 payment $400.00 to ESCROW to INTERST to fraudulently fabricate another **"default"** by the Barretts that never existed in their escrow account for Loan #11147585.

As admitted and verified by Kenig on October 23, 2018 there was never any **PAST DUE AMOUNT** of any amount for Loan #11147585 and it was Byline that was already causing the criminal fraudulent foreclosure of the Barretts' actual continuous one Property.

EXHIBIT 26 at LOT 1.com is Byline's fraudulently fabricated loan Payment Notice for Note #11147585 as dated April 2, 2018:

Principal Balance **226,409.69**
Payment Due Date **APR 16, 2018**

Your Payment Consists of

Principal	**675.70**
Interest	**779.85**
Late Charges	**105.56**
Past Due Amount	**2,727.00**
Escrow	**1,671.45**
Total Payment Due	**5,959.56**

MARCH 1, 2018 PRINCIPAL BALANCE	**227,865.24**
APRIL 2, 2018 PRINCIPAL BALANCE	**226,409.69**
	1,455.55

AGAIN: Now on April 2, 2018 Byline removed the Barretts' entire March 16, 2018 payment of $1,455.55 to **"P&I"** from the March 1, 2018 **"Your Payment Consists of"** to that fraudulently fabricated April 2, 2018 PRINCIPAL BALANCE of that $226,409.69 for Byline to fraudulently deny that the Barretts had made their March 16, 2018 payment of $1,455.55 to **"P&I"** to again fraudulently fabricate a **"default"** by the Barretts that never existed in their **"P&I"** account for loan #11147585 for Byline to cause the criminal fraudulent foreclosure of the Barretts' actual continuous one Property.

On April 18, 2018 Robert Wilson for Byline would admit and verify that all that was **"due and owing"** and **"required"** of the Barretts on April 16, 2018 was $1,455.55 for **"P&I"** under the actual provisions of loan #11147585 and not that fraudulently fabricated by Byline Total Payment Due of $5,959.56 on April 16, 2018.

Then on October 23, 2018 Kenig will admit and verify that there was never any **PAST DUE AMOUNT** of any amount for loan #11147585 and that it was Byline that was already causing the criminal fraudulent foreclosure of the Barretts' actual continuous one Property.

EXHIBIT 27 at LOT 1.com is Byline's fraudulently fabricated **PAST DUE NOTICE** for Note #11147585 as dated April 15, 2018:

DEAR CUSTOMER:

YOUR PAYMENT IS NOW ONE MONTH PAST DUE.

PRINCIPAL BALANCE	**226.409.69**
PAYMENT DUE DATE	**MAR 16, 2018**
AMOUNT OF PAYMENT	**2,832.56**
PRINCIPAL	**746.72**
INTEREST	**308.83**
LATE CHARGES	**105.56**
ESCROW	**1,671.45**
TOTAL PAST DUE	**2,832.56**

MARCH 1, 2018 PRINCIPAL BALANCE	**227,865.24**
APRIL 15, 2018 PRINCIPAL BALANCE	**226,409.69**
	1,455.55

AGAIN: Now on April 15, 2018 Byline removed the Barretts' entire March 16, 2018 payment of $1,455.55 for **"P&I"** from the March 1, 2018 **"Your Payment Consists of"** to that now fraudulently fabricated April 15, 2018 PRINCIPAL BALANCE of that $226,409.69 to fraudulently deny that the Barretts had paid on March 16, 2018 that $1,455.55 to Byline for **"P&I"** to fraudulently fabricate a **"default"** by the Barretts that never existed in their actual **"P&I"** account tor Loan #11147585 to cause the criminal fraudulent foreclosure of the Barretts' actual continuous one Property.

The Barretts' March 16, 2018 payment of $1,455.55 for **"P&I"** is now **ONE MONTH PAST DUE** and Byline can now cause the criminal fraudulent foreclosure of the Barretts' actual continuous one Property with a "default" by the Barretts that never existed.

Then on October 23, 2018 Kenig will admit and verify that there was never any **PAST DUE AMOUNT** of any amount nor at any time tor Loan #11147585 and that it was Byline that was already causing the criminal fraudulent foreclosure of the Barretts' actual continuous one Property:

SURPLUS

On April 16, 2018 the Barretts paid Byline $1,455,55 for **"P&I"** and specifically again overfunded $400.00 of escrow to their already **SURPLUS** in their actual real estate property tax escrow account for Loan #1147585 to again prevent Byline from causing the criminal fraudulent foreclosure of the Barretts actual Property.

The Barretts having done so on that April 16, 2018, then on October 23, 2018 Kenig will admit and verify that on that April 16, 2018 the balance in the Barretts' actual real estate property tax escrow account for Loan #11147585 was at least $5,833.53; that escrow account was both already **"properly funded"** , with **SURPLUS**, to both maintain Byline's REQUIRED LOW POINT BALANCE and to also already pay when due on August 1, 2018 the 2nd installment property tax bills for PIN 206 and PIN 209; there was never any PAST DUE AMOUNT of any amount for Loan #11147585; and there was no further **"Escrow"** payment of any amount for Loan #1147585 **"due and owing"** nor **"required"** of the Barretts by Byline for Loan #11147585 under the actual provisions of Loan #11147585:

SURPLUS

Pursuant to Kenig's TIMESHEET:

4/17/2018 SHK Review Cook County Assessor website for information pertaining to Westchester properties.

On that April 17, 2018 on the Assessor's website: PIN 206 was already Classification 2-12; continuous PIN 207 was already Classification 2-12; and PIN 209 was already Classification 201.

EXHIBIT 1 at LOT 1.com is that actual genuine material criminal April 18, 2018 **"demand letter"** as admitted and verified by Robert Wilson for Byline as and prepared by Kenig, which actual genuine material criminal April 18, 2018 **"demand letter"** that first Wilson and then Kenig and then Robles and then Navarro and Mitchell and Mikva all fraudulently ever existed for seven years to fraudulently deny that it was Byline that had caused the criminal fraudulent foreclosure of the Barretts' actual continuous one Property with two fraudulently fabricated **"default under the loans"** by the Barretts that never existed:

Our office has been retained by Byline Bank (the "Bank") to initiate collection proceedings with respect to the following loans (the "Loans"):

B. Statement as to Default:

Prior to taking legal action, the Bank hereby notifies you loan #11147585 is in default as a result ofthe Borrowers' failure to pay the March 16, 2018 monthly payment due and owing under Loan #11147585.

Byline's and Wilson's criminally fabricated "default" by the Barretts under Loan #11147585 never existed.

The April 18, 2018 criminal conspiracy to defraud of Byline and Wilson was to fraudulently deny that the Barretts had already made their March 16, 2018 monthly payment of $1,455.55 to **"P&I"** to criminally fabricate a **"default"** by the Barretts that never existed in the Barretts' actual Principal & Interest account for Loan #11147585 to cause the criminal accelerated foreclosure of the Barretts' actual continuous one Property as evidenced by the Barretts' actual March 16, 2018 Check Number 809 as already cashed by Byline on that same March 16, 2018.

The Bank hereby declares a default under loan #11147245 as a result of the foraging default under loan #11147585.

Byline' and Wilson's criminally fabricated **"default under loan #11147245"** never existed exactly because Byline's and Wilson's criminally fabricated **"foregoing default under Loan #111475115"** never existed as evidenced by the Barretts' March 16, 2018 Check No. 809 as already cashed by Byline on that same March 16, 2018.

C. Statement as to Amount Due:

As a result of the defaults outlined above, the Bank hereby accelerates all amounts due and owing under the loans which are now due and payable.

Byline's and Wilson's criminally fabricated "defaults outline above" never existed as evidenced by the Barretts' actual March 16, 2018 Check No. 809 as already cashed by Byline on that same March 16, 2018.

As of April 16, 2018, the total amount due and owing under the loans was as follows:

LOAN#11147585		**LOAN#11147245**	
Principal	**$226,409.69**	**Principal**	**$181, 874.13**
Interest	**1,088.68**	**Interest**	**505.46**
Late Charges	**105.56**	**Late Charges**	**0.00**
Total Amount Due	**$227,603.93**	**Total Amount Due**	**$182, 379.59**

MARCH 1, 2018 PRINCIPLE BALANCE	**227,865.24**
APRIL 16, 2018 PRINCIPLE BALNCE	**226,409.69**
	1,455.55

AGAIN: Now on April 18, 2018 Byline criminally removed the Barretts' entire March 16, 2018 payment of $1,455.55 for **"P&I"** from the March 1, 2018 **"Your Payment Consists of"** to that fraudulently fabricated April 16, 2018 PRINCIPAL BALANCE of that $226,409.69 to criminally deny that the Barretts had already made their March 16, 2018 monthly payment of that $1,455.55 to **"P&I"** to criminally fabricate a **"default"** by the Barretts that never existed in their actual Principal & Interest account for Loan #11147585; to criminally fabricate another **"default"** that never existed under Loan #11147245; to cause the criminal foreclosure of the Barretts' actual continuous one Property; for Byline to criminally seize the Barrett' actual continuous one Property for vastly below its actual then fair market value of $630,000.00.

As admitted and verified by Wilson for Byline on that April 18, 2018 after the Barretts' February 16, 2018 payment of $3,271.00 to Byline no further **"Escrow"** payment of any amount was ever **"due and owing"** nor ever **"required"** of the Barretts by Byline under the actual provisions of Loan #11147585.

Then On October 23, 2018 Kenig will admit and verify that on that April 18, 2018 the balance in the Barretts' actual real estate property tax escrow account for Loan #11147585 was at least $5,683.53; that escrow account was already both **"properly funded"**, with **SURPLUS**, to already both maintain Byline's REQUIRED LOW POINT BALANCE and also already pay the 2nd installment property taxes for PIN 206 and PIN 209 due on August 1, 2018; there was never any PAST DUE AMOUNT of any amount for Loasn #11147585; and no further **"Escrow"** payment of any amount was ever **"due and owing"** nor ever **"required"** of the Barretts by Byline for Loan #11147585 after the Barretts' February 16, 2018 payment of $3,271.00 to Byline for Loan #11147585 under the actual provisions of Loan #11147585:

SURPLUS

On that April 18, 2018, Wilson for Byline **"declared"** there was never any **"Event of Default"** of any nature in the Barretts' actual real estate property tax escrow account for Loan #11147585 under the actual provisions of Loan #11147585 exactly because there never was any **"Event of Default"** of any nature nor at any time in the Barretts' actual real estate property tax escrow account for Loan #11147585:

SURPLUS

If on March 26, 2018 Byline had not criminally removed the Barretts' entire March 16, 2018 payment of $1,455.55 to **"P&I"** from the March 1, 2018 **"Your Payment Consists of"** to that fraudulently fabricated March 26, 2018 PRINIPAL BALANCE of $226,409.69 to criminally fabricate those two **"defaults"** by the Barretts that never existed, then the Barretts would have already refinanced their actual Loans with Byline elsewhere; there is no Kenig; there is no criminal April 18, 2018 **"demand letter"**; there is no 18 CH 13221; there is no Robles; there is no criminal fraudulent foreclosure of the Barretts' actual continuous one Property; the Barretts' would not have been criminally forced into bankruptcy; there is no fraudulent public auction of the Barretts' actual continuous one Property; and the Barretts would not have been criminally evicted from their personal residence; there is no Appellate Case No 1472; and there is no Navarro and Mitchell and Mikva:

CRIMEN OMNIA EX SE NATA VITIATE OMNIA

As evidenced by the Barretts' actual March 16, 2018 Check No. 809 as cashed by Byline on that same date, the entire proceeding of both 18 CH 13221 and Appellate 1472 were already vitiated ab initio; and all of the orders and judgements as criminally entered by Judges Robles and Navarro and Mitchell and Mikva to fraudulently deny that it was Byline that had caused the criminal fraudulent foreclosure of the Barretts' actual continuous one Property were already void ab initio and of no legal force or effect for reason of the April 18, 2018 criminal conspiracy to defraud of Byline and Wilson to cause the criminal fraudulent foreclosure of the Barretts' actual continuous one Property with two fraudulently fabricated by Byline and Wilson **"defaults"** by the Barretts that never existed:

OMNIA

EXHIBIT 28 at LOT 1.com is Byline's fraudulently fabricated Loan Payment Notice for Note #11147585 as dated May 1, 2018:

Principal Balance	**225,662.97**
Payment due Date	**May 16, 2018**

Your Payment Consists of

Principal	**703.34**
Interest	**752.21**
Late Charges	**251.12**
Past Due Amount	**4,398.45**
Escrow	**1,671.45**
Total Payment due	**7,776.57**

As already admitted and verified by Wilson on April 18, 2018 all that was **"due and owing"** or **"required"** by the Barretts on May 16, 2018 under the actual provision of Loan #11147585 was $1,455.55 for Principal and Interest and not that fraudulently fabricated by Byline $7,776.57.

Then on October 23, 2018 Kenig will admit and verify that there was never any fraudulently fabricated by Byline **"Past Due Amount"** of any amount for Loan

#11147585 and it was Byline that was already causing the criminal fraudulent foreclosure of the Barretts' actual continuous one Property.

Pursuant to Kenig's TIMESHEET:

4/19/2018 SHK Telephone conference with F. Barrett, regarding loan default and issue of property taxes.

The word **"taxes"** was never in that actual genuine material criminal April 18, 2018 **"demand letter"** as already prepared by Kenig

By that actual conversation, Frank Barrett informed Kenig that the Barretts' had their cancelled March 16, 2018 check in the amount of $1,455.55 for Principal & Interest as cashed by Byline 011 that same date as the exact evidence of the April 18, 2018 criminal conspiracy defraud of Byline and Wilson to cause the criminal fraudulent foreclosure of the Barretts' actual one Property with those two fraudulently fabricated **"defaults"** by the Barretts that never existed; and explained to Kenig that the word **"Escrow"** was not in that criminal April 18, 2018 **"demand letter"** as prepared by Kenig exactly because the Barretts' personal residence and the offices has already been reclassified by the Assessor on its Website as Class 2-12.

4/23/2011 SHK Review 24 page facsimile and e-mail from F. Barrett enclosing documents showing payment of March 16, 2018 monthly installment in Loan #11147585 and explain issue regarding tax escrow. Review facsimile from F. Barrett and e-mail same to R. Wilson and outline issue regarding payment of March 16, 2018 loan installment. Review following e-mail from F. Barrett outlining further issues regarding bank's handling of loans.

Frank Barrett provided Kenig with a copy of the Barretts' March 16, 2018 Check No. 809 as marked **"#111547585 P&I"** in the amount of $1,455.55 and Kenig e-mailed same to Wilson as the exact evidence to Wilson that Byline's and Wilson's two criminally fabricated **"defaults"** never existed.

Frank Barrett also provided to Kenig the records of the Cook County Assessor and the Cook Treasurer for PIN 206 and continuous PIN 207 that the Barretts'

2017 Assessment Appeal Number 0113329 did exist; was filed with the Assessor; and had already been granted by the Assessor on its Website as of November 18, 2018:

Classification 2-12

5/4/2011 SHK Review latest e-mail from f. Barrett outlining cum:mt status of default ande-mail same to R. Wilson. Review FISERV screens from bank to recom::ile basis for loan default. Telephone conference call with R. Wilson to discuss loan default. Conforem:e call with Ft Wilson and Kohn to discuss litigation strategy in light of default based cm borrower's failure to fully fund tax escrow.

On April 18, 2018 Wilson for Byline had already admitted and verified that after the Barretts' February 16, 2018 payment of $3,271.00 to Byline for Loan #11147585 that no further **"Escrow"** payment of any amount was **"due and owing"** nor **"required"** of the Barretts by Byline for Loan #11147585 under the actual provisions of Loan #11147585 and there never was any **"Event of Default"** of any nature in the Barretts' actual real estate property tax escrow account for Loan #11147585.

On October 23, 2018 Kenig would admit and verify that on that May 4, 2018 that the balance in the Barretts' actual real estate property tax escrow for Loan #11147585 was at least $5,668.53; that escrow account was already both **"properly funded"** and **"fully funded"**, with **SURPLUS**, to both maintain Byline's REQUIRED LOW POINT BALANCE and to also pay the 2nd installment property tax bills for PIN 206 and PIN 209 when due on August 1, 2018; there was never any P**AST DUE AMOUNT** of any amount under the actual provisions of Loasn #11147585; the Barretts had paid Byline all of the monthly payments **"required"** under the actual provisions of Loan #11147585;and there never was any **"default"** of any nature nor at any time **in** the Barretts' actual real estate property tax escrow account for Loan #11147585 under the actual provisions of Loan #11147585; and the Barretts were never in any **"default"** of any nature under the actual provisions of Loan #11147585.

INSTEAD, because on April 18, 2018 Byline had failed to criminally fabricate a **"default"** by the Barretts that never existed **in** the Barretts' Principal and

Interest account for Loan #11147585 to cause the criminal fraudulent accelerated foreclosure of the Barretts' actual continuous one Property, on that May 4, 2018, Wilson and Kenig and L. Kohn criminally conspired to fraudulently fabricate a **"default"** by the Barretts that never existed in the Barretts' actual real estate property tax escrow account for Loan #11147585 to cause the criminal fraudulent foreclosure of the Barretts' actual continuous one Property:

5/7/2018 SHK Review Cook County Treasurer's website for 2016 and 2017 taxes on 1600 Westchester property.

On that May 7, 2018 those were the exact documents that **"verified"** to Kenig that the Barretts' 2017 Assessment Appeal Number 0113329 for PIN 206 did exist; was filed with the Assessor; and was already granted by the Assessor:

Classification 2-12

EXHIBIT 29 at LOT 1.com is Kenig's May 8, 2018 letter as prepared in criminal collusion with Wilson:

Re: Loan #11147585 (the "loan")

Part of the collateral for the is the real property and improvements located at 1600 Westchester Bo11!evard, Westchester, IL (the "Property"). According to the Bank's loan policies from Chicago Title, the PIN Nos. for the Property are 15-21-301- 206 and 15-21-301-209.

Kenig's fraudulently obfuscated **"Property"** is only PIN 206, which actual use is the Barretts' actual totally and attached Westchester Medical, 1600, and PIN 209, which actual use is the Barretts detached residential garage.

The last full year tax bill for the Property was 2016 at which time the aggregate real estate taxes for both PIN Nos. was $19,650.45. Figuring a modest 5.0% increase for 2017 taxes ($982,52) the estimated 2017 real estate taxes for the Property would be $20,632.98.

On October 31, 2017 the 2016 **"aggregate"** property taxes for PIN 206 and PIN 209 was that $19,650.45.

On February 13, 2018 the 2016 **"aggregate"** taxes for PIN 206 and PIN 209 was $7,266.95 due to the change in classification of PIN 206 to Classification 2-12 by the Cook County Assessor.

Figuring Kenig's modest increase of 5.0% ($363.34), on February 13, 2018 the **"estimated"** 2017 real estate taxes for PIN 206 and PIN 209 would be $7,630.29 due to the change in classification of PIN 206 to Class 2-12 and not Kenig's fraudulently fabricated $20,632.98.

On February 13, 2018 Byline had already paid a statutory total of $10,807.25 for PIN 206 and PIN 209.

Even by Kenig's obfuscation the Barretts' actual real estate property tax escrow account for Loan #11147585 was always both **"properly funded"**, with **SURPLUS**, to both already maintain Byline's REQUIRED LOW POINT BALANCE and to already also pay when due on August 1, 2018 the actual 2nd installment property taxes for PIN 206 and PIN 209.

SURPLUS

Dividing that estimate by 12 equals a monthly escrow of $1,119.41. However, as you know, the current monthly tax escrow for the loan is $1,671

However, as Kenig already knew by that actual genuine material criminal April 18, 2018 **"demand letter"** as already prepared by Kenig and as admitted and verified by Wilson, after the Barretts' February 18, 2018 payment of $3.271 to Byline for Loan #11147585 that no further **"Escrow"** payment of any amount was **"due and owing"** nor **"required"** of the Barretts by Byline for Loan #11147585 under the actual provisions of Loan #11147585.

SURPLUS

Notwithstanding, you have unilaterally decided to pay $400.00 a month toward the required real estate escrow....

Notwithstanding, on October 23, 2018 Kenig would also admit and verify that there was never any **"Past Due Amount"** of any amount nor at any time for Loan #121147585; that the Barretts had paid all of the monthly **"required"** payments for Loan #11147585; the Barretts were never in any **"default"** of any nature nor at any time under the actual provisions of Loan #111147585; and it was Byline that had caused the criminal fraudulent foreclosure of the Barretts' actual continuous one Property.

.... based upon the Certificate of Error that you filed with the Cook County Assessor seeking to change the classification from 517 (one-story commercial building) to 2-12 (mixed-use commercial/residential building).

Kenig's fraudulently fabricated **"Certificate of Error"** never existed.

Kenig's fraudulent fabrication is that what was filed with the Assessor was a **"Certificate of Error"** for PIN 206, which actual use is the Barretts' totally attached and united Westchester Medical Center, 1600, and PIN 209, which actual use in the Barretts detached residential garage.

Kenig forever fraudulently denies that the Barretts' actual 2017 Assessment Appeal Number 0113329 for PIN 206, which use is the Barretts' actual totally attached and united Westchester Medical Center, 1600, and continuous PIN 207, which actual use is the Barretts' totally attached and united personal residence, 1606, ever existed and was ever filed with the Cook County Assessor.

Although you claim in your e-mails to me that "1600 is the Westchester Medical Center office building [with PIN Nos.15-21-301-206 and 15-21=301-209] and 1606 is your personal residence [with PIN No. 15-21-301-207] .....

No such fraudulently fabricated by Kenig **"e-mails"** ever existed and Kenig's fraudulently fabricated **"separate" "Westchester Medical Center building"** never physically existed.

"I fail to see the basis for your conclusion that "1600-1606 is ONE mixed-use building."

TWO FRAUDULENTLY FABRICATED PHYSICALLY IMPOSSIBLE SEPARATE BUILDINGS

That will then become the identical fraudulently fabricated criminal absurd physically impossible frauds upon the court of first Kenig and then Robles and then Navarro and Mitchell and Mikva to fraudulently deny that PIN 206 could ever have been Class 2-12 to be assessed at 10% of market value but was always Kenig's fraudulent **"misclassification"** of Class 517 to always be assessed at 25% of market value to fraudulently deny that it was Byline that had caused the criminal fraudulent foreclosure of the Barretts' actual continuous one Property.

1600-1606 is ONE mixed-use building

SEE: 1600-1606 Westchester Boulevard

As I tried to explain to you over the phone, despite your optimism that the Assessor will grant your Certificate of Error and thereby lower the assessed value of the Property resulting in a lower tax bill ...

No such fraudulently fabricated by Kenig conversation ever existed.

Frank Barrett **"explained"** to Kenig on April 19, 2018 and then evidenced to Kenig on April 23, 2018 that the Assessor on its Website as of November 18, 2018 had already granted the Barretts' actual 2017 Assessment Appeal Number 01213329 and that both PIN 206 and continuous PIN 207 were already reclassified as Class 2-12.

On February 13, 2018 Byline had already paid the 1st installment Classification 2-12 property tax bills for PIN 206 and continuous PIN 207 as the exact evidence to Byline that the Barretts' actual 2017 Assessment Appeal Number did exist, was filed with the Assessor; and was already granted by the Assessor.

Kenig having fraudulently denied that the Barretts' actual 2017 Assessment Appeal Number 0113329 for PIN 206 and continuous PIN 207 ever existed; was ever filed with the Assessor and was already granted by the Assessor, then:

.... the basis for the Bank's calculation of the monthly escrow payment for 20111is the estimated amount of the 2017 real estate taxes. Until that estimated amount is verified to be different as determined by the Bank (which will not occur until the2nd installment of the 2017 real estate taxes are assessed) you do not have the right to adjust the monthly escrow amount.

Kenig will forever fraudulently deny that on its Website as of November 18, 2017 that the Assessor had already reduced the 2016 Final Assessed Value of PIN 206 to a 2017 Final Assessed Value of $29,019 to fraudulently deny it was Byline that was causing the criminal fraudulent foreclosure of the Barretts' actual continuous one Property.

On April 18, 2018 Wilson for Byline in that actual genuine material criminal **"demand Letter"** as prepared by Kenig had already **"verified"** to Kenig that after the Barretts' February 16, 2018 payment of $3,271.00 to Byline for Loan #11147585 that no further **"Escrow"** payment of any amount was ever **"due and owing"** nor ever **"required"** of the Barretts by Byline for Loan #11147585 under the actual provisions of Loan #11147585.

Then on October 23, 2018 Kenig will also admit and verify there was never any **"Past Due Amount"** of any amount nor of any nature nor at any time for Loan #11147585; that the Barretts had paid Byline all of the monthly **"required"** payments for for Loan #11147585 under the actual provisions of Loan #11147585; the Barretts were never in any **"default"** of any nature nor at any time under the actual provisions of their Loans with Byline; and it was Byline that had caused the criminal fraudulent foreclosure of the Barretts' actual Property.

SURPLUS

For this reason, the Bank issued the demand letter to you dated April 18,2018 declaring the Loan was in default and accelerating all sums under the Loan.

Kenig's fraudulently fabricated **"reason"** never existed.

The actual **"reason"** that Byline and Wilson had Kenig **"issue"** that actual genuine material criminal April 18, 2018 **"demand letter"** was to fraudulently fabricate two **"defaults"** by the Barretts that never existed by fraudulently denying that the Barretts had already paid their monthly payment of $1,455.55 to Byline for **"P&I"**; to cause the criminal accelerated fraudulent foreclosure of the Barretts' actual continuous one Property.

The word **"Escrow"** never occurred in that actual genuine material criminal April 18, 2018 **"demand letter"** as already prepared by Kenig.

As evidenced by that actual genuine criminal April 18, 2018 **"demand letter"** as already prepared by Kenig, Byline never **"issued"** any **"demand Letter"** for any amount of **"Escrow"** and Byline never **"declared"** any **"Event of Default"** of any nature in the Barretts' actual property tax escrow account for Loan #11147585 exactly because there was never any **"Event of Default"** of any nature in the Barretts' actual real estate property tax account for Loan #11147585 under the actual provisions of Loan #11147585.

As admitted and verified by Wilson in that actual genuine material criminal April 18, 2018 **"demand letter"** as already prepared by Kenig, no amount of **"Escrow"** was ever **"due and owing"** nor ever **"required"** of the Barretts by Byline on April 16, 2018 under the actual provisions of Loan #111547585.

The Bank stands by that demand letter.

Because that April 18, 2018 conspiracy to defraud of Byline and Wilson failed to cause the accelerated criminal fraudulent foreclosure of the Barretts' actual continuous one Property, now on May 8, 2018 Kenig just simply fraudulently fabricated an entire April 18, 2018 **"demand letter"** that never existed; to criminally fabricate another **"default"** by the Barretts that never existed; to criminally make it impossible for the Barretts to refinance their actual Loans prior to maturity.

In the meantime, despite the confirming default under the loan, so long as the monthly principal and interest payments of $1,455.55 continue to be paid along with the monthly escrow amount of $400.00 (which the Bank continues to dispute), tile Bank has decided at this time to delay exercising its rights and remedies under tile Loan as a result of the foregoing default.

Kenig's fraudulently fabricated **"foregoing default"** never existed.

If the Barretts caused a **"default"** then the Barretts had to pay Kenig's Legal Fees.

If Byline caused a **"default"** Byline had to pay Kenig's Legat Fees.

Wilson and Kenig wanted the Barretts to continue to pay Byline $400.00 per month and therein admit that the Barretts had caused a **"default"**.

The loans must be paid in full at the stated maturity on September 21, 2018. Failure to do so will result in an event of default under the Loans at which time, if not sooner as outlined above, the Bank will exercise any and all of its rights

under the loans including institution of suit(s) to collect the loans, foreclose on the Mortgages or any other necessary action.

"if not sooner as outlined above"

That is exactly how Byline criminally made it impossible for the Barretts to refinance their actual Loans with Byline elsewhere prior to maturity.

If the Barretts attempted to refinance their actual Loans with Byline elsewhere prior to maturity, Byline would simply file a COMPLAINT FOR FORECLOSURE in criminal furtherance of the two **"default under the loans"** by the Barretts that never existed.

cc. Robert Wilson (via electronic mail only)

That is the exact same Wilson who had already admitted and verified in that actual genuine material criminal April 18, 2018 **"demand Letter"** as already prepared by Kenig that there was never any **"Event of Default"** of any nature in the Barretts actual real estate property tax escrow account for Loan #11147585 and it was Byline that was causing the criminal fraudulent foreclosure of the Barretts' actual continuous one Property:

APRIL 18, 2018 OCCURRED BEFORE MAY 8, 2018

CRIMEN OMNIA EX SE NATA VITIATE

OMNIA

EXHIBIT 30 at LOT 1.com is Byline's fraudulently fabricated **PAST DUE NOTICE** for Note #11147585 as dated May 15, 2018:

DEAR CUSTOMER:
YOUR PAYMENT IS NOW TWO MONTHS PAST DUE

PRINCIPAL BALANCE	**225,662.**
PAYMENT DUE DATE	**MAR 16, 2018**
AMOUNT OF PAYMENT	**1,552.57**
PRINCIPAL	**0.00**
INTEREST	**0.00**

LATE CHARGES	**251.12**
ESCROW	**1,271.45**
TOTAL PAST DUE	**4,649.57**

On April 18, 2018 the exact criminal conspiracy to defraud of Byline and Wilson was that the Barretts had failed to make their March 16, 2018 monthly payment of $1,455.55 to **"P&I"** to fraudulently fabricate two **"defaults"** by the Barretts that never existed to cause the criminal fraudulent accelerated foreclosure of the Barretts' actual continuous one Property.

NOW, on May 15, 2018 Byline put the Barretts' exact March 16, 2018 payment of $1,455.55 to **"P&I"** back into the Barretts' **"P&I"** account for Note #11147585 to fraudulently deny that actual genuine material criminal April 18, 2018 **"demand letter"** as prepared by Kenig ever existed.

The May 15, 2018 criminal conspiracy to defraud now is that the Barretts failed to make their March 16, 2018 monthly **"ESCROW"** payment of that $1,271.45 to criminally fabricate those two **"defaults under the loans"** by the Barretts that never existed to criminally make it impossible for the Barretts to refinance their actual Loans with Byline prior to maturity.

Byline criminally fabricated that May 15, 2018 **PAST DUE NOTICE** for Note #11147585 to exactly criminally match Kenig's fraudulently fabricated May 8, 2018 letter.

Then on October 23, 2018 Kenig will admit and verify that there was never any **"PAST DUE AMOUNT"** of any amount for Loan #11147585 and that it was Byline that was causing the criminal fraudulent foreclosure of the Barretts' actual continuous one Property.

Exactly because on April 18, 2018 that Wilson had admitted and verified that after the Barretts' February 16, 2018 payment of $3,271.00 to Byline that no further **"Escrow"** payment of any amount was ever **"due and owing"** nor **"required"** of the Barretts by Byline for Loan #11147585, on May 16, 2018 the Barretts ceased overfunding their real estate property tax account for Loan #11147585 and paid Byline only $1,455.55 for **"P&I"**.

On Kenig's TIMESHEET Wilson and Kenig were very upset that the Barretts did not pay Byline $400.00 for Escrow and the Barretts in doing so denied they were ever any of Kenig's fraudulently fabricated **"defaults"** that never existed.

EXHIBIT 31 at LOT 1.com is Byline's fraudulently fabricated Loan Payment Notice for Note #11147585 as dated June 3, 2018:

Principal balance **225,662.92**
Payment Due Date **JUN 16, 2018**

Your Payment Consists of

Principal **678.26**
Interest **771.29**
Late Charges **396.69**
Past Due Amount **6,069.90**
Escrow **1,671.45**
Total Payment Due **9,593.58**

As already admitted and verified by Wilson in that actual genuine material criminal April 18, 2018 **"demand Lette**r" as already prepared by Kenig, all that was **"due and owing"** of the Barretts to Byline on June 16, 2018 was $1,455.55 for Principal & Interest and not that fraudulently fabricated by Byline $9,593.58.

Then on October 23, 2018 Kenig would admit and verify that there never was any **"Past Due Amount"** of any amount for Loan #11147585 and it was Byline that was causing the criminal fraudulent foreclosure of the Barretts' actual continuous one Property by criminally preventing the Barretts from refinancing their actual Loans with Byline elsewhere prior maturity.

On June 16, 2018 the Barretts paid Byline $1,455.55 for Principal & Interest.

EXHIBIT 32 at LOT 1.com is Byline's fraudulently fabricated **PAST DUE NOTICE** for Note #11147585 as dated June 17, 2018:

DEAR CUSTOMER:
YOUR PAYMENT IS NOW TWO MONTHS PAST DUE

PRINCIPAL BALANCE **225,662.97**
PAYMENT DUE DATE **APR 16, 2018**

AMOUNT OF PAYMENT	**3,339.55**
PRINCIPAL	**675.75**
INTEREST	**595.75**
LATE CHARGES	**396.68**
ESCROW	**1,671.45**
TOTAL PAST DUE	**9,953.68**

Then on October 23, 2018 Kenig would admit and verify that there was never any **"PAST DUE AMOUNT"** of any amount for Loan #11147585 and that it was Byline that was causing the criminal fraudulent foreclosure of the Barretts actual continuous one Property by criminally preventing the Barretts from refinancing their actual loans with Byline elsewhere prior to maturity.

On June 20, 2018 the Barretts paid First Secure & Trust Bank $1,000.00 for due diligence to refinance loan #11147585. Then Wintrust would use that due diligence to refinance loan #11147245.

EXHIBIT 33 at LOT 1.com is Byline's fraudulently fabricated loan Payment Notice for Note #11147585 as dated July 2, 2018:

Principal Balance	**224,987.27**
Payment Due Date	**JUL 16, 2018**

Your Payment Consists of

Principal	**705.11**
Interest	**750.11**
Late Charges	**542.24**
Past Due Amount	**7,741.35**
Escrow	**1,671.45**
Total Payment Due	**11,410.59**

On April 18, 2018 Wilson had already admitted and verified that alt that was **"due and owing"** by the Barretts to Byline on July 16, 2018 was $1,455.55 for Principal and Interest and not that fraudulently fabricated by Byline $11,410.59.

Then on October 23, 2018 Kenig will admit and verify that there was never any **"Past Due Amount"** of any amount for Loan #11147585 and it was Byline that was causing the criminal fraudulent foreclosure of the Barretts actual continuous one Property

EXHIBIT 34 at LOT 1 is Kenig's letter to the ARDC as dated July 3, 2018:

The dispute with Mr. Barrett involves Loan #111475115 which requires monthly principal and interest payments in the amount of $1,455.55 along with a monthly tax escrow payment of $1,671.45 which is based 011 the estimated 2917 real estate taxes for the Property of $20,057.40. The real estate taxes for the Property in 2016 were $19,650.45.

Kenig's fraudulently fabricated **"dispute"** never existed.

On April 18, 2018 Wilson had already admitted and verified in that actual genuine material criminal April 18, 2018 **"demand letter"** as already prepared by Kenig that after the Barretts' February 16, 2018 payment of $3.271.00 to Byline for Loan #1114585 that no further **"Escrow"** payment of any amount was **"required"** of the Barretts by Byline for Loan #11147585 under the actual provisions of Loan #11147585.

Based on the foregoing, the monthly payment for Loan #11147585 is $3,271.00 ($1,455.55 + $1,671.45. On March 16, 2018, instead of paying the Bank the required monthly installment of $3,271.IJO, Mr. Barrett paid the Bank $1,1155.55 representing principal and interest payment in the amount of $1,455.55 and a tax escrow payment of $400.00.

The exact April 18, 2018 criminal conspiracy to defraud of Byline and Wilson was that the Barretts had failed to pay that exact March 16, 2018 payment of that exact $1,455.55 to P&I to criminally fabricate two **"defaults"** by the Barretts that never existed to cause the criminal fraudulent accelerated foreclosure of the Barretts' actual continuous one Property.

Kenig just admitted such:

APRIL 18, 2018 OCCURRED BEFORE MAY 8, 2018

CRIMEN OMNIA EX SE NATA VITIATE

OMNIA

As a result of Mr. Barrett's failure to pay the required monthly installment payment under Loan #11147585, the Bank requested that I issue a demand

letter (the "Demand Letter") to the borrowers. I did so on April 18, 2018. A copy of the Demand Letter is enclosed.

Kenig's now fraudulently fabricated April 18, 2018 **"Demand letter"** never existed.

The now July 3, 2018 criminal conspiracy to defraud of Byline and Kenig, which will then become the identical criminal frauds upon the court of Kenig and then Judges Robles and then Navarro and Mitchell and Mikva, is that the Barretts failed to make their March 16, 2018 **"required"** monthly installment payment of $1,271.45 to Byline to criminally fabricate those two **"default under the Loans"** by the Barretts that never existed to criminally deny that it was Byline that had caused the criminal fraudulent foreclosure of the Barretts' actual continuous one Property.

The word **"Escrow"** never occurred in that actual genuine material criminal April 18, 2018 **"demand Letter"** as already prepared by Kenig:

APRIL 18, 2018 OCCURRED BEFORE MAY 8, 2018

CRIMEN OMNIA EX SE NATA VITIAT

OMNIA

The bottom line here is that Mr. Barrett has defaulted under the terms of the loans ....

Those two fraudulently fabricated by Kenig **"defaulted under the terms of the loans"** by the Barretts that never existed made it criminally impossible for the Barretts to refinance their actual Loans with Byline elsewhere prior to maturity.

Then on October 23, 2018 Kenig will admit and verify those two fraudulently fabricated **"defaulted under the terms of the loans"** never existed and that it was Byline that had caused the criminal fraudulent foreclosure of the Barretts' actual continuous one Property:

SURPLUS

EXHIBIT 35 at LOT 1.com is the actual genuine material Cook County 2017 Second Installment Property Tax Bill for PIN 206 as issued on that same July 3, 2018, which Kenig and then Robles and then Navarro and Mitchell and Mikva fraudulently deny ever existed to fraudulently deny that it was Byline that had caused the criminal fraudulent foreclosure of the Barretts' actual continuous one Property:

Classification 2-12

The TOTAL PAYMENT DUE is $0.00; the 2017 Assessment Level is 10%, the 2016 Assessed Value of $63,025 has been adjusted to a 2017 Assessed Value of $29,019; and the 2016 Total Tax of $18,380.95 has been reduced to a 2017 Total Tax of $6,643.29.

Then this is the already conspiracy to defraud of Byline and Kenig which will then become the identical criminal frauds upon the court of Kenig and then Robles and then Navarro and Mitchell and Mikva:

FACTS	FIX
Cook County Assessor	**Kenig/Robles/Mitchell/Mikva**
ONE MIXED USE BUILDING	**TWO SEPARATE BUILDING**
Classification 2-12	**Classification 517**
2016 Total Tax $18,380.95	**2016 Total Tax $18,380.95**
TOTAL PAYMENT DUE $0.00	**TOTAL PAYMENT DUE $9,279.15**
2016 Assessed Value 63,025	**20616 Assessed Value $63,025**
2017 Assessment Level 10%	**2017 Assessment Level 25%**
2017 Assessed Value 29,019	**2017 Assessed Value 72,547**
2017 Total Tax 6,643.29	**2017 Total Tax 19,388.67**

Kenig and then Judges Robles and then Navarro and then Mitchell and Mikva fraudulently deny that PIN 206 was ever Classification 2-12 to be assessed at 10% of market value but was always Kenig's fraudulent **"misclassification"** of Classification 517 to always be assessed at 25% of market value; to deny the TOTAL PAYMENT DUE was $0.00 but was a fraudulently fabricated TOTAL PAYMENT DUE of $9,279.95; fraudulently denied that the 2016 Assessed Value of $63,025 was ever reduced to a 2017 Assessed Value of $29,019 but had increased to a fraudulently fabricated 2017 Assessed Value of $72,547; to fraudulently deny that the 2016 Total Tax of $18,380.95 was ever reduced to a 2017 Total Tax of $6,643.29 but had increased to a fraudulently fabricated 2017 Total Tax of $19,388.67 to fraudulently fabricate a **"default"** by the Barretts that never existed in their actual real estate property tax account for Loan #11147585 for Byline to criminally prevent the Barretts from refinancing their actual Loans with Byline elsewhere prior to maturity.

On October 23, 2018 Kenig will admit and verify that on that July 3, 2018 the actual balance in the Barretts' real estate property tax escrow account for Loan #111547585 was: $5,683.53.

EXHIBIT 36 at LOT 1.com is the Cook County Treasurer 2017 Second Installment Property Tax Bill for PIN 209, which actual use is the Barretts' detached residential garage as paid by Byline on July 13, 2018:

TOTAL PAYMENT DUE

$566.28

On that July 13, 2018 the Barretts were entitled to and received $3,466.23 from the Cook County Treasurer for the OVERPAYMENT of the 2017 property taxes for PIN 206.

Then this is the already criminal conspiracy of Byline and Kenig to cause the criminal fraudulent foreclosure of the Barretts' actual continuous one Property:

LOAN #11147585

PIN 206: Classification 2-12

ESCROW BALANCE		**$5,683.53**
PIN 206 TOTAL PAYMENT DUE	**=**	**$0.00**
PIN 209 TOTAL PAYMENT DUE	**=**	**$566.28**
REQUIRED LOW POINT BALANCE	**=**	**$3,275.09**
SURPLUS		**$1,842.16**

With PIN 206 being Classification 2-12 on July 3, 2018 the Barretts' actual real estate property tax escrow account was already both **"properly funded"**, with **SURPLUS**, to both already maintain Byline's REQUIRED LOW POINT BALANCE and to also pay the actual 2nd installment property tax bills for PIN 206 and PIN 209 when due on August 1,2018 and there was never in any **"Event of Default"** at anytime in the Barretts' actual real estate property tax escrow account for Loan #11147585:

SURPLUS $1,842.16

LOAN #11147585

PIN 206: Classification 517

ESCROW BALANCE		**$5,683.53**
PIN 206 TOTAL PAYMENT DUE	=	**$9,845.43**
PIN 209 TOTAL PAYMENT DUE	=	**$566.28**
REQUIRED LOW POINT BALANCE	=	**$3,275.09**
		$8,003.27

With PIN 206 always being Kenig's fraudulent **"misclassification"** of Class 517 to always be assessed at 25% of market value, then the Barretts real estate property tax escrow account for Loan #11147585 was not **"properly funded"** on July 3, 2018 to pay when due the 2nd installment property tax for Loan #11147585, the exact criminal intent of Kenig's fraudulent **"misclassification"** of Class 517 to always be assessed at 25% of market value to criminally fabricate those two **"default under the Loans"** by the Barretts that never existed to criminally make it impossible for the Barretts to refinance their actual Loans with Byline prior to maturity.

DEFICIT:$8,003.27

On July 14, 2018 the Barretts paid Byline $1,455.55 for Principal & Interest for Loan #11147585.

EXHIBIT 37 at LOT 1.com is Byline's fraudulently fabricated **PAST DUE NOTICE** for Note #11147585 as dated July 15, 2018:

DEAR CUSTOMER:
YOUR PAYMENT IS NOW THREE MONTHS PAST DUE.

PRINCIPAL BALANCE	**224,987.27**
PAYMENT DUE DATE	**APR 16, 2018**
PRINCIPAL	**0.00**
INTEREST	**0.00**
LATE CHARGES	**542.24**
ESCROW	**1,487.35**
TOTAL PAST DUE	**8,283.59**

On April 18, 2018 the criminal conspiracy to defraud of Byline and Wilson was that the Barretts had failed to pay their monthly payment of $1,455.55 to **"P&I"** to criminally fabricate two **"defaults"** by the Barretts that never existed to cause the criminal fraudulent accelerated foreclosure of the Barretts' actual continuous one Property.

Now on July 15, 2018 Byline put the Barretts's entire March 16, 2018 payment of $1,455.55 to **"P&I"** back into the Barretts' Principal & Interest account for Loan #11147585 to fraudulently deny that actual genuine material criminal April 18, 2018 **"demand letter"** as prepared by Kernig ever existed.

On October 23, 2018 Kenig would admit and verify that there was never any **"PAST DUE AMOUNT"** of any amount for Loan #11147585 and that it was Byline that was causing the criminal fraudulent foreclosure of the Barretts' actual continuous one Property with Kenig's fraudulently fabricated **"misclassification"** of PIN 206 having always been Classification 517 to always have been assessed at 25% of market value.

Pursuant to Kenig's TIMESHEET

8/11/2018 SHK Site visit to property in preparation for meeting with Cook County Assessor regarding PIN number discrepancies.

1600-1606 is ONE mixed-use building
SEE: 1606 Westchester Boulevard

Kenig's TIMESHEET exactly already admitted all of Kenig's and then Judges Robles's and then Navarro's and Mitchell's and Mikva's criminal identical fraudulently fabricated physically impossible frauds upon the court before Kenig and then Robles and then As admitted and verified by Wilson on April 18, 2018, all that was **"required"** of the Barretts on August 16, 2018 under the actual provision of Loan #1212147585 was $1,455.55 for Principal & Interest and not that fraudulently fabricated by Byline $13,227.86.

Then on October 23, 2018 Kenig will admit and verify that there was never any **"Past Due Amount"** of any amount for Loan #11147585 and it was Byline that was causing the criminal fraudulent foreclosure of the Barretts' actual continuous one Property with Kenig's fraudulently fabricated **"misclassification"** of PIN 206 always being Classification 517 to always be assessed at 25% of market value.

On August 16, the Barretts paid Byline $1,455.55 for Principal & Interest for Loan #11147585.

Pursuant to the actual genuine material records of the Cook County Assessor; the Cook County Treasurer and Byline's actual records for Loan #11147585 with the 2017 classification of PIN 206 being Classification 2-12, the actual PAYOFF for Loan #11147585 due on September 21, 2018 was:

Prinicpal	**$222,219.73**
Interest	**897.26**
Escrow	**(5,117.25)**
	$217,999.65

On August 20, 2018 the Barretts were formally approved by e-mail by First Bank & Trust to refinance Loan #11147585 subject to what was actually owed Byline; mandatory appraisal; customary closing costs; and a simultaneous closing with Wintrust to refinance Loan #11147245.

EXHIBIT 39 at LOT 1.com is Byline's fraudulently fabricated Loan Notice for Note #11147585 as dated September 6, 2018 and in exact criminal furtherance of Kenig's fraudulent **"misclassification"** of PIN 206 always being Classification 517 to always be assessed at 25% of market value:

Principal Balance	**$224,315.73**
Payment Due Date	**SEP 21, 2018**

Your Payment Consist of

Principal Balance	**$222,219.64**
Interest	**897.26**
Late Charges	**545.42**
Past Due Amount	**11,088.25**
Escrow	**1,671.45**
Total Payment Due	**$236, 418.02**

There never were any fraudulently fabricated by Byline **"Late Charges"** for Loan #11147585.

There never was any fraudulently fabricated by Byline **"Past Due Amount"** of any amount for Loan #11147585.

There was never any fraudulently fabricated by Byline **"Escrow"** due on September 21, 2018.

That fraudulently fabricated by Byline **"YOUR PAYMENT IS NOW THREE MONTHS PAST DUE"** for Loan #11147585 that never existed; those fraudulently fabricated by Byline **"Late Charges"** of $545.42 that never existed; that fraudulently fabricated by Byline **"Past Due Amount"** of that $11,088.25 that never existed for Loan #11147585; and that fraudulently fabricated **"Escrow"** that was never due on September 21, 2018; and that fraudulently fabricated by Byline **"Total Payment Due"** of that $236,418.02 criminally made it impossible for the Barretts to refinance their actual Loans with Byline elsewhere prior to maturity, the exact criminal intent of Kenig's fraudulent **"misclassification"** of PIN 206 always being Classification 517 to always be assessed at 25% of market value.

Kenig's fraudulent **"misclassification"** of PIN 206 always being Class 517 to always be assessed at 25% became those two fraudulently fabricated by Kenig **"default under the loans"** by the Barretts that never existed.

Kenig's fraudulent **"misclassification"** of PIN 206 always being Classification 517 to always be assessed at 25% of assessed value was the exact cause of 18 CH 123221.

That was the exact criminal intent of Kenig's fraudulent **"misclassification"** of PIN 206 always being Classification 517 to always be assessed at 25% of market value.

Byline having criminally made it impossible for the Barretts to refinance their actual Loans with Byline elsewhere prior to maturity with those two fraudulently fabricated by Kenig **"default under the Loans"** by the Barretts that never existed, then on October 23, 2018 Kenig filed Byline's fraudulent COMPLAINT FOR FORECLOSURE AND OTHER RELIEF for Loan #112147585.

EXHIBIT 39 at LOT 1.com is Page 3 of that fraudulent COMPLAINT:

The Note is in default for reason of non=payment of sums at maturity. As of September 25, 2018, the indebtedness has not been paid, and the following sums (excluding default interest and Legal fees) remained due and owing under the Note and the Mortgage:

Principal Balance	***$224,315.73***
Interest	***3,299.37***
Late charges	***545.65***
Escrow Balance	***(5,117.25)***
Total Due	***$223,043.21***

As already prepared by Byline, the Interest due on September 21, 2018 was $897.26 and not that as fraudulently fabricated now by Byline $3,299.37.

There never was any as fraudulently fabricated by Byline **"Late Charges"** tor Loan #11147585.

There was never any fraudulently fabricated by Byline **"DEFICIT"** in the Barretts' actual real estate property tax escrow account tor Loan #11147585.

There was never any **"PAST DUE AMOUNT**" of any amount for Loan #11147585 under the actual provisions of Loan #11147585.

The Barretts paid all of their monthly **"required"** payments to Byline under the actual provision of Loan #11147585.

The Barretts were never in any **"default"** of any nature under the actual provisions of Loan #11147585.

On that October 23, 2018 Kenig exactly admitted and verified that after the Barretts' February 16, 2018 payment of $3,271.00 to Byline that the Barretts' actual real estate property tax escrow account for Loan #111147585 was both already **"properly funded"**, with **SURPLUS**, to both already maintain Byline' REQUIRED LOW POINT BALANCE and also to already pay the actual 2017 property taxes for PIN 206 and PIN 209; there was never any **"PAST DUE AMOUNT"** of any amount for Loan #11147585; the Barretts had paid to Byline all of their monthly **"required"** payments under the actual provisions of Loan #11147585' the Barretts were never in any two fraudulently fabricated by Kenig "default under the loans" of any nature nor at any time under the actual provisions of Loan #111147585; and it was Byline that had caused the criminal fraudulent foreclosure of the Barretts' actual continuous one Property by criminally making it impossible for the Barretts to refinance their actual Loans with Byline elsewhere prior to maturity with those two fraudulently fabricated by Kenig **"default under the loans"** by the Barretts that never existed:

SURPLUS $1,842.16

Escrow Balance (5,115.25)

Kenig on that October 23, 2018 having admitted that it was Byline that had caused the criminal fraudulent foreclosure of the Barretts' actual continuous one Property with those two fraudulently fabricated by Byline **"default under the Notes"** by the Barretts that never existed, then the following are the identical criminal frauds upon the court of first Kenig and then Judges Robles and then Navarro and Mitchell and Mikva to specifically fraudulently deny that actual genuine material criminal April 18, 2018 **"demand letter"** prepared by Kenig ever existed; and particularly fraudulently deny that PIN 206 was ever Classification 2-12 to be assessed at 10% of market value; and then the criminal fraud upon the court of Cook County Judge Thomas Donnelly to all criminally deny that it was Byline that had caused the criminal fraudulent foreclosure of the Barretts' actual continuous one Property.

These are the actual genuine material Legal Descriptions of the Barretts' actual Mortgages with Byline as submitted by Kenig **"multiple times"** in the record of an entirely vitiated 18 CH 13221 by Kenig:

LOT 1 EXCEPT THE SOUTH 34.23 FEET AND THE VACATED ALLEY LYING WEST OF AND ADJOINING IN GEORGE F. NIXON AND COMPANY'S CENTRAL ADDITION TO WESTCHESTER, BEING A SUBDIVISION OF ....
PIN No. 15-21-301-206-0000

PIN 206 is the Barretts' actual totally attached and united Westchester Medical Center, 1600.

THE EAST 35 FEET AND THE EAST 35 FEET OF THE NORTH 25 FEET OF LOT 5 IN ISABLE, A SUBDIVISION IN .....
PIN No. 15-21-301-209-0000

PIN 209 is the Barretts actual detached residential garage

THE SOUTH 34.23 FEET OF LOT 1 AND VACATED ALLEY LYING WEST OF AND ADJOINING SAID SOUTH 34.23 FEET OF LOT 1 IN GEORGE F. NIXON AND COMPANY' CENTRAL ADDITION TO WESTCHER, BEING A SUBDIVION OF ....
PIN No.15-231-301=207-0000

PIN 207 is the Barretts' actual totally attached and united personal residence, 1606.

On April 15, 2018 Kenig filed Byline's fraudulent MOTION FOR APPOINTMENT OF RECEIVERSHIP for the fraudulent procurement of a Receiver to further prevent the Barretts from refinancing their actual Loans with Byline elsewhere.

Byline demanded a June 19, 2018 hearing for the fraudulent procurement of that Receiver.

At Barretts' DEFENDANTS' RESPONSE TO PLAINTIFF'S MOTION FOR APPOINTMENT OF RECEIVER is the sworn AFFIDAVIT of Frank Barrett:

My residence and the offices are contained in 1 building located on:

Lot 1 in George F. Nixon & Company's Central Addition to Westchester, being a Subdivision of ....

Because of Kenig's May 8, 2018 letter, the Barretts submitted the actual genuine material Plat of Survey for the Barretts' actual continuous one Property with the actual legal description of the Barretts' actual continuous one Property evidencing that the Barretts' totally attached and united **"four sided"** 1600-1606 was always entirely located on that 100 foot wide Lot 1 East of that Vacated Alley:

The WARRANTY DEED with the actual legal description of the Barretts' actual continuous one Property:

The Cook County Assessor BUILDING RECORD RESIDENTIAL for 1606 with the diagram of 1600 being totally attached and united to 1606 as one **"four sided"** mixed-use building:

Q-UP 2-12 w/4068#

Four pictures of the Barretts' **"four-sided"** totally attached and united 1600-1606.

And plead one roof, common wall; adjoining interior door; and located on Lot 1.

The Barretts particularly evidenced the December 30, 2014 letter from the Village of Westchester as demanded by and provided to Byline for the 2015 renewal of the Barretts' Loans with Byline:

The property located at 1606 Westchester Boulevard is zoned B-1 Office Building District. The property is improved with a one-story structure that has medical/ dental offices and a residence on it. The structure was constructed ii April 1954. Professional offices are currently a permitted use. Residential uses are currently permitted above the first floor. The property is legal non-conformingwith respect to the residential use on the first floor.

At Byline's May 29, 2019 REPLY BRIEF IN SUPPORT OF ITS MOTION FOR RECEIVERSHIP:

(h) The Village of Westchester considers the property to be one structure with medical/dental offices and a residence on it.

Contrary to the Borrowers' belief the facts support the contention that the two buildings are separate and not one structure.

TWO FRAUDULENTLY FABRICATED PHYSICALLY IMPOSSIBLE SEPARATE BUILDINGS

Kenig's fraudulently fabricated physically impossible **"facts"** could never have existed.

1600=1606 is ONE mixed-use building

SEE: 1600-1606 Westchester Boulevard

Further in that REPLY BRIEF as stated by Kenig and as already plead by the Barretts:

(e)There is a single roof for the entire building.

Since the two buildings are contiguous and each one-story, it is not surprising that there is a single roof. That fact is likely more indicative that the two buildings were constructed at the same time.

Further in that REPLY BRIEF:

The Sidwell map for Cook County, attached hereto as Exhibit E, also shows that the two buildings are on separate, distinct lots. The commercial building sits

on lot "206" and the residential building sits on lot "207". A clearer picture of that same Sidwell map appears on Page 12 of the appraisal attached hereto as Exhibit F.

That actual genuine material **"Page 12"** is already EXHIBIT 4 at LOT 1.com

Kenig exactly evidenced that the Barretts' totally attached and united **"four sided"** 1600- 1606 is located entirely on that 100 foot wide Lot 1 East of that Vacated Alley.

Kenig's fraudulently fabricated **"Sidwell map of Cook County"** never existed; Kenig's fraudulently fabricated "Exhibit E" never existed; Kenig fraudulently fabricated **"two buildings"** never existed; Kenig's fraudulently fabricated **"separate, distinct lots"** never existed; Kenig's fraudulently fabricated **"commercial building"** never existed; Kenig's fraudulently fabricated "lot "206" never existed; Kenig's fraudulently fabricated "residential building" never existed; and Kenig's fraudulently fabricated "lot "207" never existed.

Kenig fraudulently misrepresented PIN 206 for property taxation purposes only to fraudulently fabricate that **"Lot 206"** that never existed; to fraudulently fabricate that **"commercial building"** that never existed; and fraudulently misrepresented continuous PIN 207 for property taxation purposes only as that fraudulently fabricated **"Lot 207"** that never existed; to fraudulently fabricate that "residential building" that never existed; to fraudulently deny that Lot 1 ever existed; to fraudulently deny that PIN 206 was ever Classification 2-12 to be assessed at 10% but was always Kenig' s fraudulently **"misclassification"** of Clas 517 to always be assessed at 25% of market value to fraudulently deny that it was Byline that had caused the criminal fraudulent foreclosure of the Barretts' actual continuous one Property.

At Page 10 of that REPLY BRIEF is the culmination of all of Kenig's fraudulently fabricated physically impossible criminal frauds upon the court:

Each building has its own address
Each building has its own entries
Each building has its own legal description
1Each building has its own parcel number

Each building has its own city lot
Each building is separately metered for water and electric
Each building could be sold separately

The Property is currently being marketed for rent to potential commercial research users. The exact reason for all of Kenig's fraudulently fabricated criminal physically impossible frauds upon the court is to forever fraudulently deny that PIN 206 was ever Classification 2- 12 to be assessed at 10% of market value but was always Kenig's fraudulent **"misclassification"** of Class 517 to always be assessed at 25% of market value to fraudulently deny that it was Byline that had caused the criminal fraudulent foreclosure of the Barretts' actual continuous one Property.

Typical Kenig, EXHIBIT 40 at LOT 1.com is Page 13 of the RESTRICTED APPRAISAL of the Barretts' actual totally attached and united four sided 1600-1606 as ordered by Byline:

Real Estate Tax Data (2017 taxes payable in 2018)

TAX PARCEL NUMBER	2017 REAL ESTATE TAXES
Property #1	
15-21-301-206	**$6,643.29**
15-21-301-209	**$1,264.80**

The exact fraudulent intent of all of Kenig's criminally fabricated physically impossible frauds upon the, which will then become the identical criminally fabricated physically impossible frauds upon the court of Robles and Navarro and Mitchell and Mikva, is that PIN 206 could never have been Class 2-12 to be assessed at 10% of market value but was always Kenig's fraudulent **"misclassification"** of Class 517 that was always Class 517 to always be assessed at 25% of market value to fraudulently deny that it was Byline that had caused the criminal fraudulent foreclosure of the Barretts' actual continuous one Property.

By that Page 13, Kenig exactly admitted that the Barretts' 2017 Assessment Appeal Number 0113329 for PIN 206 and continuous PIN 207 did exist; was filed with the Assessor; and was granted by the Assessor; the 2017 classification of PIN 206 was Class 2-12; PIN 206 was assessed at 10% of market value; and Byline did cause the criminal fraudulent foreclosure of the Barretts' actual continuous one Property with Kenig's fraudulent **"misclassification"** of PIN 206 always being Class 517 to be assessed at 25% of market value

Pursuant to Kenig's TIMESHEET

6/1/2019 SHK Revise proposed receivership order.

On that June 1, 2019 Kenig **"revised"** that "proposed receivership order" because Byline had changed the proposed Receiver.

EXHIBIT 41 at LOT 1.com is the forever void criminal fabricated physically impossible ORDER APPROVING RECEIVER FOR NON-RESIDENTIAL PROPERTY as already prepared on June 1, 2019 by Kenig and then criminal entered by a clueless Judge Robles on June 19, 2019:

THE COURT FINDS:

At Paragraph 1:

Copies of the mortgage and assignment of rents are attached to the complaint, ... against the property identified above.

Pursuant to the Legal Descriptions of both that Mortgage and that Assignment of Rents:

LOT 1 EXCEPT THE 34.23 FEET AND THE VACATED ALLEY LYING WEST AND ADJOINING IN GEORGE F. NIXON AND COMPANY'S CENTRAL ADDITION TO WESTCHESTER, BEING A SUBDIVISION ....

On October 23, 2018 Kenig had already evidenced all of Kenig's fraudulently fabricated physically impossible frauds upon the Court with the actual genuine material Legal Descriptions of both the Mortgage and the Assignments of Rents before Kenig even committed Kenig's fraudulently fabricated physically impossible frauds upon the court.

2. **The property is improved with a one-story medical office building that is owned by the defendants-mortgagors and is not for use as defendant(s)/mortgagor(s) personal property.**

TWO FRAUDULENTLY FABRICATED PHYSICALLY IMPOSSIBLE SEPARATE BUILDINGS

As evidenced herein, that is Kenig's already handwriting in Paragraph 5.

At Paragraph 10, no THE COURT FINDS comes with FILL IN THE BLANK FORMS

At Paragraph 13 and 15, no THE COURT FINDS ever contains FILL IN THE BLANK FORMS

SHK

Those were never **THE COURT FINDS** of Robles as ever **"rendered"** by clueless Robles **AFTER** that June 19, 2019 hearing as demanded by Byline for the fraudulent procurement of that Receivership.

As evidenced herein by Kenig's handwriting, those are Kenig's fraudulently fabricated physical impossible **THE COURT FINDS** of Kenig as already prepared by Kenig on June 1, 2019 BEFORE that June 19, 2019 hearing as demanded by Byline for the fraudulent procurement of that Receivership.

All clueless Robles had to do on that June 19, 2019 was to say what Robles had AGREED with Byline what Robles was told to say by Byline BEFORE that June 19, 2019 hearing as demanded by Byline for the fraudulent procurement of that Receiver; and then just criminally enter WHATEVER Kenig put in front of clueless Robles by Kenig as already prepared by Kenig on June 1, 2019.

On that June 19, 2019, Robles was absolutely clueless as to what clueless Robles was criminally entering for Byline, nor did clueless Robles have to worry for one second in doing so because of the Cook County Appellate Court and the Illinois Supreme Court.

6/19/2019 SHK E-mail to receiver enclosing receivership order.

On September 21, 2021, Kenig, the already maker of those fraudulently fabricated physically impossible June 19, 2019 **THE COURT FINDS**, was kind enough to explain to clueless Robles just exactly what clueless Robles criminally entered on that June 19, 2019:

As noted above, on June 19, 2019 this Court granted Byline's motion to appoint a receiver for the 1600 Property resulting in the Barretts filing for bankruptcy. Following the dismissal of that bankruptcy case, the Barretts, on several occasions, have expressed their dissatisfaction with the Court's ruling appointing a receiver contending that the Court was wrong to conclude that the 1600 Property is separate from the 1606 Property. In fact, the entire impetus of the Barretts is that the properties consist of "one mixed-use building", a refrain that the Barretts repeat throughout the Motion.

"separate"

That was never any fraudulently fabricated by Kenig **"Court's ruling"** as ever **"rendered"** by clueless Robles AFTER that June 19, 2019 hearing as demanded by Byline for the fraudulent procurement of that Receivership.

Kenig's **"1600 Property"** is Kenig's fraudulently fabricated physically impossible **"Lot 206".**

Kenig's **"1606 Property"** is Kenig's fraudulently fabricated physically impossible **"Lot 207".**

What was criminally entered by that clueless Robles on that June 19, 2019 was Kenig's forever criminal fraudulently fabricated physically impossible fraud upon the court of:

The Sidwell map of Cook County. Exhibit E attached to, also shows that the two building are on separate, distinct lots. The commercial building sits on Lot "206" and the residential building sits on Lot "207".

On July 1, 2019 the fraudulently procured Receiver took criminal possession of the Barretts' totally attached and united Westchester Medical Center, 1600, and its rentals for now Kenig and Robles to criminally make it further impossible for the Barretts to refinance their actual Loans with Byline elsewhere.

On July 11, 2019 the Barretts filed their AFFIRMATIVE DEFENSE and COUNTER CLAIM FOR DAMAGES.

On July 15, 2019 the Barretts were criminally forced into bankruptcy by Kenig and Robles by that fraudulently procured Receivership.

EXHIBIT 42 at LOT 1.com as part of that bankruptcy proceeding as criminally caused by Kenig and Robles and provided to the Barretts by Byline is Byline's Loan Year-To-Date Activity for Note #11147585 as dated 12/31/2019:

	Principal	**Escrow**
END OF PREVIOUS YEAR BALANCE	**$223,563,53**	**$5,117.25**

Byline's COMPUTER admitted and verified that after the Barretts' February 16, 2018 payment of $3,271.00 to Byline for Note #11147585 that the Barretts actual real estate property escrow account for Note #11147585 was already both "properly funded", with **SURPLUS,** to both maintain Byline's REQUIRED LOW POINT BALANCE and to also pay when due on August 1, 2018 the actual 2nd installment real estate property tax bills for PIN 206 and PIN 207; there was never **any"PAST DUE AMOUNT"** of any amount nor at anytime for Note #11147585 under the actual provisions of Note #11147575; the Barretts paid Byline all of the Barretts' monthly **"required"** payments under the actual provisions of Loan #11147585; the Barretts were never in any **"default"** of any nature nor at any time under the actual provisions of Note #11147585; and it was Byline that had caused the criminal fraudulent foreclosure of the Barretts' actual continuous one Property by criminally making it impossible for the Barretts' to refinance their actual Loans with Byline prior to maturity with two fraudulently fabricated **"default under the loans"** by the Barretts that never existed:

SURPLUS: $1,842.16

Escrow Balance ***(5,117.25)***

Then these are the October 25, 2021 criminal frauds upon the court of Robles striking the Barretts' MOTION TO VACATE THE ENTIRE PROCEEDING AND VACATE ALL ORDERS FOR REASON OF PHYSICALLY IMPOSSIBLE FRAUDS UPON THE COURT for Robles to fraudulently deny that it was Byline that had caused the criminal fraudulent foreclosure of the Barretts' continuous one Property:

On June 19, 2019, after extensive argument on the record with both Plaintiff's Counsel and Counsel for the Barretts present, this Court appointed a Receiver over the 1600 Property which consists of a 1-story office building which is leased out to tenants. The Order entered by this Court on that date specifically set forth that Order does not ap the 1606 Property which consists of a 1-story single-family residence.

AFTER

Those were never Robles's THE COURT FINDS **"rendered"** by Robles **"AFTER"** that June 19, 2019 hearing as demanded by Byline for the fraudulent procurement of a Receiver.

Robles's **"1600 Property"** is now Kenig's fraudulently fabricated physically impossible **"Lot 206"**.

Robles's **"1606 Property"** is now Kenig's fraudulently fabricated physically impossible **"Lot 207"**.

What was criminally entered by clueless Robles on that June 19, 2019 was Kenig's criminally fabricated physically impossible fraud upon the court of:

The Sidwell map of Cook County, attached herein as Exhibit E, also shows that the two buildings are on separate, distinct lots. The commercial building sits on Lot"206" and the residential building sits on Lot"207".

Further in that void ORDER is the fate of ALL of the Motions filed by the Barretts:

On July 11, 2019 the Barretts filed their Answer, (6) one-sentence Affirmative Defense and (4) counter claims under five different theories of recovery. All of the affirmative defenses and counter claims were stricken by this Court on Plaintiff's motions.

ALL

Further in that forever void ORDER:

The allegations against Plaintiff and its Counsel seem to arise from a dispute about the amount of tax escrow payments the Barretts were required to make under the loan documents versus what the Barretts were actually paying.

No such fraudulently fabricated first by Kenig and now Robles **"tax escrow" "dispute"** ever existed under the actual provisions of Loan #11147585.

It appears that on or about April 18, 2018, the Barretts decided they were going to start making escrow payments Less than the required amount under the loan documents. This, in part led to a letter of default sent to the Barretts on April 18,2018.

As evidenced by that actual genuine material criminal April 18, 2018 **"demand letter"** as prepared by Kenig, on that April 18, 2018 no amount of **"Escrow"** was ever **"due and owing"** nor ever **"required"** of the Barretts by Byline under the actual provisions of Loan #11147585.

The word **"Escrow"** never occurred in that actual genuine material criminal April 18, 2018 **"demand letter"** as prepared by Kenig.

A letter dated May 8, 2018 from the Plaintiff's counsel sent to the Barretts set forth, in part, the reason the April 11!, 2011! letter was sent. Specifically, that letter stated the default arose, in part, from the Barretts "unilateral" decision to reduce the monthly escrow payments from $1,671.45 to $400.00 per month based on the Barretts' efforts to have their properties reclassified from commercial to single mixed use.

"properties"

First Kenig's and now Robles's fraudulently fabricated **"reason"** never existed.

The actual "reason" that Byline and Wilson had Kenig issue that actual genuine material criminal April18, 2018 "demand Letter" was for Byline and Wilson to fraudulently deny that the Barretts had already made their March 16, 2018 payment to Byline for Loan #11147585of $1,455.55 for "P&I"; to criminally fabricate a **"default"** by the Barretts that never existed in their actual "P&I" account for Loan #11147585; to criminally fabricate another **"default"** under Loan #11147245; to criminally cause the criminal fraudulent foreclosure of the Barretts' actual continuous one Property.

When the Barretts produced their March 16, 2018 Check No. 809 in the amount of $1,455.55 specifically marked "#11147585" and as already cashed by byline on that same March 16, 2018, then on May 8, 2018 Kenig criminally fabricated another **"default"** by the Barretts that never in the Barretts' actual real estate property tax escrow account for Loan #11147585 to exactly criminally prevent the Barretts from refinancing their actual Loans with Byline elsewhere prior to maturity.

The word **"Escrow"** never occurred in that actual genuine material April 18, 2018 **"demand letter"** as prepared by Kenig; Byline never **"issued"** any **"demand letter"** for **"Escrow"** of any amount for Loan #11147585; and Byline never **"declared"** any **"Event of Default"** of any nature nor at any time in the Barretts' actual real estate property tax account for Loan #11147585; exactly because there was never any **"Event of Default"** of any nature nor at any time in the Barretts' actual real estate property tax escrow account for the Barretts' Loan #11147585:

APRIL 18, 2018 OCCURRED BEFORE MAY 8, 2018

CRIMEN OMNIA EX SE NATA VITIAT

OMNIA

Robles having criminally denied that actual genuine material criminal April 18, 2018 **"demand letter**" as prepared by Kenig ever existed to criminally deny that it was Byline that had caused the criminal fraudulent foreclosure of the Barretts' actual continuous one Property, then further in that forever void ORDER:

The issue of alleged "misclassification" of Property as discussed by the Defendants dose not establish a "fraudulent foreclosure" let alone defeat the instant foreclosure action. Though the Barretts MAY have achieved a reclassification of their properties from commercial to "single mixed-use" this Court agrees with Plaintiff that has nothing to do with the allegations made in the complaint relating to the alleged default under the loans in question.

"properties"

Prior to that June 19, 2019 hearing as demanded by Byline for the fraudulent procurement of that Receiver **"this Court"** had already **AGREED** with Plaintiff to criminally enter **WHATEVER** the already prepared by Kenig on June 1, 2019 THE COURT FINDS of Kenig put in front of **"this Court"** by Kenig.

As already admitted and verified by Kenig on October 23, 018, there was never any PAST DUE AMOUNT of any amount nor at anytime for Loan #11147585 under the actual provisions of Loan #1114758; and it was Kenig's fraudulently fabricated **"misclassification"** of PIN 206 always being Class 517 to always be assessed at 25% of market value that had caused the criminal fraudulent foreclosure of the Barretts' actual continuous one Property.

Robles committed all of Robles's criminal frauds upon the court to criminally deny that it was Byline that had caused the criminal fraudulent foreclosure of the Barretts' actual continuous one Property:

AFTER

On October 23, 2018 Kenig had already admitted and verified that it was Byline that had caused the criminal fraudulent foreclosure of the Barretts' actual continuous one Property with Kenig's fraudulently fabricated **"misclassification"** of PIN 206 always being Classification 517 to always be assessed at 25% of market value:

SURPLUS: $18,642.16

Escrow Balance (5,117.25)

At Kenig's December 27, 2021 is Byline's REPLY BRIEF IN SUPPORT OF ITS MOTION FOR SUMMARY JUDGEMENT:

According to the demand letter, Note Ii was in default as a result of the Barretts' failure to pay the March 16, 2018 monthly Installment due and owing under Note II. This default also resulted in a default under Note 1. As a result of the foregoing defaults, Byline accelerated all amounts due and owing under the Notes.

Kenig's evidenced fraud upon the court is that the Barretts failed to pay their March 16, 2018 payment of **$1,277.45** to **"Escrow"** for Loan #11147585 to cause a **"default"** by the Barretts that never existed in their actual real estate property tax account for Loan #1114758 to criminally fabricate another **"default"** by the Barretts that never existed under Loan #11147245 to criminally prevent the Barretts from refinancing their actual Loans with Byline prior to maturity.

The Barretts contend that they paid the principal andinterest due on March 16, 2018 ...

The exact April 18, 2018 criminal conspiracy to defraud of Byline and Wilson was that the Barr

The exact April 18, 2018 criminal conspiracy to defraud of Byline and Wilson was that the Barretts had failed to pay Byline their March 16, 2018 monthly payment of $1,455.55 to **"P&I"** to criminally fabricate a **"default"** by the Barretts that never existed in their **"P&I"** account for Loan #11147585; to criminally fabricate another **"default"** that never existed under Loan #11147245; to cause the criminal fraudulent accelerated foreclosure of the Barretts' actual continuous one Property.

..... but they admit that they refused to pay the required tax escrow because they filed a tax appeal and the assessor was going to reduce the assessed value thereby reducing the monthly tax escrow amount. As of March 18, 2018 that was not the case and the Barretts had no right to unilaterally refuse to pay the monthly tax escrow account which is why Byline declared Note II in default.

As admitted and verified by Wilson in that actual genuine material criminal April 18, 2018 **"demand letter"** as prepared by Kenig and then as admitted by Kenig on October 23, 2018, after the Barretts' February 16, 2018 payment to Byline of $3,271.00 for Loan #11147585 no further **"Escrow"** payment of any amount was ever **"due and owing"** nor ever **"required"** of the Barretts for Loan #11147585 under the actual provisions of Loan #11147585; and there was no **"Escrow"** payment of any amount ever **"due and owing"** nor ever **"required"** of the Barretts by Byline on March 16, 2018:

As evidenced by that actual genuine material criminal April 18, 2018 **"demand letter"** as prepared by Kenig, on April 18, 2018 Byline and Wilson criminally **"declared"** a **"default"** by the Barretts in their **"P&I"** account that never existed by criminally denying that the Barretts had already paid Byline on March 16, 2018 their monthly installment payment of $1,455.55 for **"P&I"** to criminally **"declare"** another **"default"** under Loan #11147585 that never existed to cause the criminal fraudulent accelerated foreclosure of the Barretts' actual continuous one Property.

The word **"Escrow"** never occurred in that actual genuine material criminal April 18, 2018 **"demand letter"** as prepared by Kenig.

Byline never **"issued"** any **"demand letter"** of any amount of **"Escrow"** for Loan #11147585 and Byline never **"declared"** any **"Event of Default"** of any nature in the Barretts' actual real estate property tax escrow account for Loan #11147585; exactly because there never was any **"Event of Default"** of any nature in the Barretts' actual real estate property tax account for Loan #111547585.

Consequently, not only were the Notes in default on April 18, 2018 as outlined in the demand letter, but they were also in default at the time the complaint was filed due to maturity.

Consequently, the word **"Escrow"** never occurred in that actual genuine material criminal April 18, 2018 **"demand letter"** as prepared by Kenig.

Consequently, as evidenced by the Barretts' actual March 16, 2018 Check Number 809 as already cashed by Byline on that same March 16, 2018 and that actual genuine material criminal April 18, 2018 **"demand letter"** as prepared by Kenig, the Barretts were never in any criminally fabricated by Kenig **"Notes in default"** of any nature; and it was Kenig's fraudulently fabricated **"Notes in default"** that never existed that had caused the criminal fraudulent foreclosure of the Barretts' actual continuous one Property by criminally making it impossible for the Barretts to refinance their actual Loans with Byline elsewhere prior to maturity:

APRIL 18, 2018 OCCURRED BEFORE MAY 8, 2018

CRIMEN OMNIA EX SE NATA VITIAT

OMNIA

Kenig having fraudulently denied that actual genuine criminal April 18, 2018 **"demand letter"** as prepared by Kenig ever existed to fraudulently deny that it was Byline that had caused the criminal fraudulent foreclosure of the Barretts' actual continuous one Property, then further in that REPLY BRIEF:

Receivership Order

The majority of the Barretts' Response and Addendum continues to rehash the Barretts' dissatisfaction with the Court's entry of the continue to think that the Receivership Order, which was outlined above, is long since moot. While

the Barretts continue to think that the 1600 Property and the 1606 Property are one building, the Court, long ago, based on the facts presented to this Court at the Receivership hearing concluded that the 1600 Property and the 1606 Property are two separate buildings, with the former being occupied by commercial tenants and the latter consisting of the Barretts' personal residence.

"two separate buildings"

That **"Receivership Order"** was never **THE COURT FINDS** of Robles **AFTER** that June 19, 2019 **"Receivership hearing"** as demanded by Byline for the fraudulent procurement of that Receiver.

As evidenced by Kenig's handwriting, that was Kenig's fraudulently fabricated physically impossible **"Receivership Order"** of Kenig as already prepared by Kenig on June 1, 2019.

What was criminally entered by clueless Robles on that June 19, 2019 was Kenig's fraudulently fabricated physically impossible fraud upon the court of:

The Sidwell map of Cook County, attached herein as Exhibit E, also shows that the two buildings are 011 separate, distinct lots. The commercial building sits on Lot "206" and the residential building sits on Lot "207".

Kenig committed all of Kenig's criminal fraudulently fabricated physically impossible frauds upon the court to fraudulently deny that it was Byline that had caused the criminal fraudulent foreclosure of the Barretts' actual continuous one Property:

AFTER

On October 23, 2018 that Kenig had already admitted and verified that it was Byline that had caused the criminal fraudulent foreclosure of the Barretts' actual continuous one Property:

SURPLUS: $1,842.16

Escrow Balance (5,117.25)

EXHIBIT 43 at LOT 1.com is the forever void February 10, 2022 ORDER as already prepared by Kenig and then criminally entered by Robles wherein Byline is granted summary judgement on EVERYTHING; judgement is entered against the Barretts for $457,976.33; the Barretts have to pay Kenig's Legal Fees of $80,766.80; and the fraudulent public auction of the Barretts' actual continuous one Property is ordered, all because the Barretts' totally attached and united **"four sided"** totally attached and united 1600-1606 as always located on LOT 1 was always Kenig's and now Robles criminally fabricated physically impossible:

T**he Sidwell map of Cook County, attached hereto as Exhibit E, also shows that the two buildings are on separate, distinct lots. The commercial building sits on Lot "206" and the residential building sits on Lot "207".**

EXHIBIT 44 at LOT 1.com is the fraudulent NOTICE OF SALE for the fraudulent public auction of the Barretts' actual continuous one Property as prepared by Kenig and dated May 16, 2022;

LOT 1 EXCEPT THE SOUTH 34.23 FEET ...

THE SOUTH 34.23 FEET OF LOT 1

On June 26, 2022 Byline won the fraudulent public auction of the Barretts' actual continuous one Property with a bid of$394,096.

EXHIBIT 45 at LOT 1.com is the forever void JUDICIAL SALE DEED as prepared by Kenig and dated July 25, 2022:

LOT 1 EXCEPT THE SOUTH 34.23 FEET ....

THE SOUTH 34.23 FEET Of LOT ....

Kenig had that void JUDICIAL SALE DEED assigned to an Arete Investments Fund IV, LLC with Kenig as the Agent for both Byline and Arete.

Arete immediately offered the Barretts' actual continuous one Property for $630,000.00 while at the exact same time Kenig claimed the Barretts' actual continuous one Property had a fair market value of $400,000.00

EXHIBIT 46 at LOT 1.com is the forever void ORDER APPROVING REPORT OF SALE AND DISTRIBUTION, CONFIRMING SALE, AND ORDER FOR POSSESSION as already prepared by Kenig and then criminally entered by Robles as dated December 19, 2022:

LOT 1 EXCEPT THE SOUTH 34.23 FEET ......

THE SOUTH 34.23 FEET OF LOT 1 ......

The real property located at 1600 Westchester Boulevard, Westchester, Illinois 60154 that is the subject matter of this proceeding consists of a one-story office building with on-site parking and the real property located at 1606 Westchester Boulevard, Westchester, Illinois 60154 that is also the subject matter of this proceeding consists of a one-story single-family home (collectively "the Properties). The successful purchaser or holder of the Certificate of Sale is entitled to possession of the Properties only.

"Properties"

That is Kenig's forever fraudulently fabricated physically impossible fraud upon the court of:

The Sidwell map of Cook County, attached hereto as Exhibit E, also shows that the two buildings are on separate, distinct lots. The commercial building sits on Lot "206" and the residential building sits on Lot "207".

Summary judgement in the amount of $170,522.01 is entered against the Barretts; Arete is granted possession of the Barretts' totally attached and united Westchester Medical Center, 1600, and the Cook County Sherriff is ordered to evict the Barretts from their totally attached and united personal residence, 1606.

At Byline's RESPONSE BRIEF to the Barretts' MOTION TO RECONSIDER that forever void ORDER as criminally entered by Robles on that December 19, 2022:

The Restricted Appraisal Report was ordered by Byline in connection with the filing of the lawsuit on October 23, 2018. It was Exhibit F of Byline's reply brief in support of its motion to appoint a receiver filed on May 29, 2019. The Restricted Appraisal Report was attached to the reply brief for the sole purpose of supporting Byline's argument that the subject property contained two buildings and two separate lots for the purpose of Byline's motion to appoint a receiver for one of the buildings.

Specifically, the reply brief stated:

The Sidwell map of Cook County, attached hereto as Exhibit E, also shows that the two buildings are on separate, distinct lots. The commercial building sits on lot "296" and the residential building sits on lot "207".

EXHIBIT 47 at LOT 1.com is Robles's forever void denying the Barretts' MOTION TO RECONSIDER that void December, 2019 ORDER as criminally entered by Robles and dated July 21, 2023:

The Court finds that the Barretts' motion fails to set forth any legally recognizable basis for the Court to reconsider entry of this Court of this Court's order entered on December 19, 2022 approving the report of sale and distribution relating to the properties which are the subject of this litigation. Therefore, the motion to reconsider is hereby DENIED.

"properties"

Robles's **"properties"** are Kenig's forever fraudulently fabricated criminal frauds upon the court of:

The Sidwell map of County, attached hereto as Exhibit E, also shows that the two buildings are on separate, distinct lots. The commercial building sits on lot "206" and the residential building sits on lot "207".

On August 25, 2023 the Barretts filed their NOTICE OF APPEAL: Case Number 1472.

On that August 25, 2023 the Barretts already had full knowledge beyond any shadow of any doubt that three Cook County Appellate Court Judges would commit the exact same frauds upon the Appellate Court of Kenig and Robles to criminally protect the criminal judicial corruption of Robles by criminally affirming all of the criminal summary judgements as criminally entered by Robles against the Barretts and the Barretts acted accordingly:

THE REPUTATION OF THE COOK COUNTY APPELLATE COURT PROCEDES ITSELF

On that same August 25, 2023 Kenig executed an EVICTION ORDER with the Cook County Sherriff to have the Barretts evicted from their totally attached and united personal residence, 1606.

On December 19, 2023, with Kenig present, Arete criminally seized the Barretts' totally attached and united Westchester Medical Center, 1600, only to find 1600 was VACANT for reason of the fraudulent foreclosure.

On January 18, 2024 with Kenig present the Cook County Sherriff came to 1606 to criminally evict the Barretts from their personal residence only to find that the Barretts had already vacated 1606 to save their personal belongings.

EXHIBIT 48 at LOT 1.com is Kenig's entire February 19, 2024 APPELLATE REPLY BRIEF:

STATEMENT OF FACTS

The 1600 Property consists of a 1-story medical office building that was owned by the Elarretts and leased to several tenants.

Kenig's **"1600 Property"** is Kenig's fraudulently fabricated physically impossible **"separate, distinct" Lot"206"**.

The 1606 Property consists of a 1-story single-family residence that was occupied by the Barretts.

Kenig's **"1606 Property"** is Kenig's fraudulently fabricated physically impossible **"separate, distinct" Lot"207"**.

"any other security in the Properties"

"sale as to both Properties:

"Sale of the Propertied occurred"

"argued that the Properties"

"nature of the underlying Properties"

"fair market value of the "Properties"

"whether the Properties were"

"value of the Properties"

"liquidation of the Properties"

"aggregate appraised value of the Properties"

Those were Kenig's fraudulently fabricated physically impossible frauds upon the Appellate Court of:

The Sidwell map of Cook County, attached hereto as Exhibit E, also shows that the two buildings are on separate, distinct lots. The commercial building sits on Lot "206" and the residential building sits on lot "207".

Kenig committed all Kenig's criminal fraudulently fabricated physically impossible frauds upon the Appellate Court to fraudulently deny that PIN 206 was ever Classification 2-12 to be assessed at 10% of market value but was always Kenig's fraudulently fabricated **"misclassification"** of PIN 206 always being Classification 517 to always be assessed at 25% of market value to fraudulently deny that it was Byline that had caused the criminal fraudulent foreclosure of the Barretts' actual continuous one Property:

AFTER

Kenig on October 23. 2018 had already admitted and verified that it was Byline that had caused the criminal fraudulent foreclosure of the Barretts' actual continuous one Property:

SURPLUS: $1,846.16

Escrow Balance (5,117.25)

ARGUMENT

A. The existence of a default:

Throughout the entire brief, the Barretts complain that a default never occurred under the Notes. As outlined above, Note I matured on September 21, 2018 and Note II matured on September 16, 2018 after which Byline filed Foreclosure Action. Byline alleged the existence of the default in the Complaint and proved this fact as part of its motion for summary judgement which the Court granted on February 8, 2022.

The actual genuine material Legal Descriptions of the Barretts' actual Mortgages with Byline as attached to those Complaints by Kenig exactly evidenced all of Kenig's fraudulently fabricated physically impossible frauds upon the court before Kenig even committed Kenig's fraudulently fabricated physically impossible frauds upon the court:

LOT 1 EXCEPT THE SOUTH 34.23 FEET ....

THE SOUTH 34.23 FEET OF LOT .....

Notwithstanding, the Barretts ignore the foregoing defaults and instead argue that the default declared in Byline's default letter dated April 18,2018 was fraudulent. The basis for the default letter was the Barretts failure to pay the monthly installment under Note II which also triggered a default under Note 1.

The actual **"basis"** of that actual genuine material criminal April 18, 2018 **"demand letter"** as prepared by Kenig was that the Barretts failed to pay their March 16, 2018 monthly installment of $1,455.55 to **"P&I"** to fraudulently fabricate a **"default"** by the Barretts that never existed in the Barretts' actual **"P&I"** account for Loan #11147585; to fraudulently fabricate another **"default"** that never existed under Loan #11147245; for Byline to cause the criminal fraudulent accelerated foreclosure of the Barretts' actual continuous one Property.

Kenig's now fraud upon the Appellate Court is that the Barretts failed to pay their March 16, 2018 monthly installment of $1,217.25 to **"Escrow"** for Kenig to now fraudulently fabricate a **"default"** by the Barretts in their real estate property tax escrow account for Loan #11147585; to fraudulently fabricate another **"default"** that never existed under Loan %11147245; for Kenig to fraudulently deny that it was Byline that had caused the criminal fraudulent foreclosure of the Barretts' actual continuous one Property.

In spite of the Barretts' contention, both defaults occurred under the Notes and it was not until the Barretts failed to pay the amounts due and owing at maturity that Byline decide to file the Foreclosure Action.

As evidenced by that actual genuine material criminal April 18, 2018 **"demand letter"** as prepared by Kenig and the Barretts' actual March 18, 2018 Check No. 809 as already cashed by Byline on that same March 126, 2018, those criminally fabricated by Kenig **"defaults under the Notes"** never existed; and it was those two fraudulently fabricated by Kenig **"defaults under the Notes"** that never existed that had criminally made it impossible for the Barretts to refinance their actual Loans with Byline elsewhere prior to maturity.

Thus, the Barretts' argument throughout this case that a default never existed was correctly rejected multiple times by the trial court and should be ignored by this Court.

"multiple times, Robles fraudulently denied that actual genuine material criminal April 18, 2018 **"demand letter"** as prepared by Kenig ever existed to fraudulently deny that it was Byline that had caused the criminal fraudulent foreclosure of the Barretts' actual continuous one Property.

APRIL 18, 2018 OCCURRED BEFORE MAY 8, 2018

CRIMEN OMNIA EX SE NATA VITIAT

OMNIA

Kenig committed all of Kenig's criminal fraudulently fabricated frauds upon the Appellate Court to criminally deny that it was Byline that had caused the criminal fraudulent foreclosure of the Barretts' actual continuous one Property:

AFTER

On October 23, 2018 Kenig had already admitted and verified that it was Byline that had caused the criminal fraudulent foreclosure of the Barretts' actual continuous one Property:

SUR.PLUS: $1,842.16

Escrow Balance (5,117.25)

EXHIBIT 49 at LOT.com is the entire void March 22, 2024 ORDER as delivered ny Justice Navarro. Justice Mitchell and Justice Mikva concurred:

The 1600 Westchester property consisted of a one-story medical office building that was owned by the Barretts and leased to several tenants.

That **"property"** is Kenig's fraudulently fabricated physically impossible **"separate, distinct" "Lot 206"** that never existed.

The 1606 Westchester property consists of a one-story single-family residence that was occupied by the Barretts.

That **"property"** is Kenig's fraudulently fabricated physically impossible **"separate, distinct" "Lot 207"** that never existed.

"judicial sale of the properties"

"concerning the two properties"

"tax bill for the 1600 and 1606 properties"

"get the properties reclassified"

"for both properties in default"

"foreclosure and sale of both properties"

"judicial sale of the properties"

That were Kenig's fraudulently fabricated physically

Those were Kenig's fraudulently fabricated physically impossible frauds upon the court of:

The Sidwell map of Cook County, attached hereto as Exhibit E, also shows thar the two buildings are on separate, distinct lots. The commercial building sits on Lot "206" and the residential building sits on lot "207".

Navarro and Mitchell and Mikva committed their fraudulently fabricated physically impossible frauds upon the court to forever fraudulently deny that PIN 206 was ever Classification 2-12 to be assessed at 10% of market value but was always Kenig's fraudulent **"misclassification"** of PIN 206 always being Classification 517 to always be assessed at 25% of market value to fraudulently deny that it was Byline that had caused the criminal fraudulent foreclosure of the Barretts' actual continuous one Property:

AFTER

On October 23, 2018 Kenig had already admitted and verified that it was Kenig's fraudulently **"misclassification"** of PIN 206 always being Class 517 to always be assessed at 25% of market value that had caused the criminal fraudulent foreclosure of the Barretts' actual continuous one Property:

SURPLUS: $1,842.16

Escrow Balance (5,117.25)

Further in that void ORDER:

Here, the Barretts' main contention in their motion to dismiss, and on appeal, appears to be that Byline committed fraud when it issued the May 8, 2018 letter notifying the Barretts of their default and preventing the Barretts from refinancing their Loans elsewhere before the notes expired. However, this remains a legal conclusion unsupported by specific facts.

"main contention"

Even Kenig had admitted in that actual fraudulent May 8, 2018 letter:

For this reason, the Bank issued a demand letter to you dated April 18, 2018 declaring the Loan in default and accelerating all sums due and owing under the loan.

Navarro and Mitchell and Mikva still fraudulently denied that actual genuine material criminal April 18, 2018 **"demand Letter"** as prepared by Kenig ever existed because that fraudulently fabricated by Kenig **"default"** by the Barretts in their real estate property tax escrow account never existed "under the Loan" as exactly evidenced by that actual genuine material criminal April 18, 2018 **"demand letter"** as already prepared by Kenig.

SIXTEEN TIMES the Barretts cited that actual genuine material criminal April 18, 2018 **"demand letter"** as prepared by Kenig as the Barretts' **"main contention"** that the Barretts were never in any **"default"** of any nature under the actual provisions of the Barretts' Loans with Byline and that it was Byline that had caused the criminal fraudulent foreclosure of the Barretts' actual continuous one Property.

Even Kenig had already admitted in Kenig' Appellate Brief

Throughout there entire brief, the Barretts complain that a default never occurred under the Notes.

Notwithstanding, the Barretts ignore the foregoing defaults and instead argue that the default letter dated April 18,2018 was fraudulent.

APRIL 18, 2018 OCCURRED BEFORE MAY 8, 2018

Even pathological liars Kenig and Robles admitted the existence of an April 18, 2018 **"demand Letter"** as prepared by Kenig but just fraudulently denied that actual genuine material criminal April 18, 2018 **"demand letter"** as prepared by Kenig ever existed to fraudulently deny that it was Byline that had caused the criminal fraudulent foreclosure of the Barretts' actual continuous one Property.

Now Judges Navarro and Mitchell and Mikva have taken being pathological liars to new heights, even by Cook County Appellate Court standards, by criminally denying that actual genuine criminal April 18, 2018 **"demand letter"** as prepared by Kenig ever even existed to criminally deny that it was Byline that had caused the criminal fraudulent foreclosure of the Barretts' actual continuous one Property by criminally preventing the Barretts from refinancing their actual Loans with Byline elsewhere prior to maturity.

Exactly because of the reputation of the Cook County Appellate Court, SIXTEEN TIMES the Barretts cited that actual genuine material criminal April 18, 2018 **"demand letter"** as prepared by Kenig as their "main contention" that it was Byline that had caused the criminal fraudulent foreclosure of the Barretts' actual continuous Property just so three Cook County Appellate Court Judges could **SIXTEEN TIMES** commit identical criminal fraud upon the court of fraudulently deny that actual genuine material criminal April 18, 2018 **"demand letter"** as prepared by Kenig ever existed to fraudulently deny that it was Byline that had caused the criminal fraudulent foreclosure of the Barretts' actual continuous one Property:

SIXTEEN TIMES: IT WAS ALL THAT SIMPLE

That void March 22, 2024 ORDER is self-explanatory.

Navarro and Mitchell and Mikva just simply repeated all of Kenig' fraudulent fabrications in Kenig' May 8, 2018 letter and cited all of Robles's criminal frauds upon the court to criminally deny that it was Byline that had caused the criminally deny that it was Byline that had caused the criminal fraudulent foreclosure of the Barretts' actual continuous one Property:

AFTER

Kenig on October 23, 2018 had already admitted and verified that it was Byline that had caused the criminal fraudulent foreclosure of the Barretts' actual continuous one Property:

SURPLUS: $1,842.16

Escrow Balance (5,117.25)

Further in that void March 22, 2024 ORDER:

The Barretts' brief contains 38 pages of "facts" that are riddled with arguments about fraud and fabrications.

"facts"

This is afterthe criminal frauds upon the Appellate Court and fraudulent fabrications of Judges Navarro and Mitchell and Mikva to fraudulently deny that it was Byline that had caused the criminal fraudulent foreclosure of the Barretts' actual continuous one Property:

APRIL 18, 2018 OCCURRED BEFORE MAY 8, 2018

CRIMEN OMNIA EX SE NATA VITIAT

OMNIA

Based upon the identical criminal frauds upon the Appellate Court of Kenig and Judges Navarro and Mitchell and Mikva to fraudulently deny that it was Byline that had caused the criminal fraudulent foreclosure of the Barretts' actual continuous one Property. On July 3, 2024 the Barretts filed a COMPAINT FOR DAMAGES FOR FRAUDULENT FORECLOSURE AND OTHER RELIEF and a SUMMONS for a mandatory September 4, 2024 court appearance by Byline: Presiding Judge Thomas Donnelly: Case 2024L007310: Calendar W.

Exhibit 1 of that COMPLAINT was that actual genuine material criminal April 18, 2018 **"demand Letter"** prepared by Kenig that Kenig and then Robles and then Navarro and Mitchell and Mikva criminally conspired for years to deny ever existed to fraudulently deny that it was Byline that had caused the criminal fraudulent foreclosure of the Barrett's actual contentious one Property.

Exhibit 2 of that COMPLAINT was the Barretts' actual March 16, 2018 Check No. 809 in the amount of $1,455.55 as specially marked **"#11147585 P&I"** as already cashed by Byline on that same March 16, 2018 as the exact evidence that Byline had caused the criminal fraudulent foreclosure of the Barretts' actual continuous one Property:

CRIMEN OMNIA EX SE NATA VITIAT

OMNIA

EXHIBIT 50 at LOT 1.com is the SHERRIFF'S OFFICE OF COOK COUNTY AFFIDAVIT OF SERVICE as served on a JESSICA GAMBOAof Byline on July 30, 2024.

Byline had 30 days to file an APPEARANCE or an ANSWER.

By September 4, 2024 Byline did not file an APPEARANCE nor an ANSWER and Byline was not Court on that September 4, 2024.

As such, without having read the Barretts' COMPLAINT, Judge Donnelly found Byline in "default".

EXHIBIT 51 at LOT 1.com is the September 4, 2024 ORDER as entered by Judge Donnelly for a PROVE UP hearing for October 18, 2024 as prepared by Judge Donnelly's Clerk.

The Barretts provided those requisite documents for that October 18, 2024 hearing as verified by Judge Donnelly's Clerk.

Frank Barrett was personally in Judge Donnelly's Courtroom for that October 18, 2024 PROVE UP hearing.

Judge Donnelly immediately informed Frank Barrett that now Judge Donnelly had read the Barretts' COMPLAINT which accused Judges Robles and then Navarro and Mitchell and Mikva of criminally conspiring to deny that it was Byline that had caused the criminal fraudulent foreclosure of the Barretts' actual one Property with identical criminal frauds upon the court:

CRIMEN OMNIA EX SE NATA VITIAT

OMNIA

That was the first sign of trouble.

All of a sudden, Kenig, who for seven years had fraudulently denied that actual genuine criminal April 18, 2018 **"demand letter"** as prepared by Kenig ever existed, appeared by ZOOM; purported to be Byline's Attorney; fraudulently denied a SUMMONS was ever served on Byline; and accused the Barretts of fraud.

Judge Donnelly presented to Kenig the SHERRIFF'S AFFIDAVIT that the SUMMONS was served on that Jessicca Gamboa of Byline on July 30, 2024 and Kenig still accused the Barretts of fraud.

Inspite of Kenig's fraud, or rather in criminal furtherance of Kenig's fraud, Judge Donnelly insisted that Kenig prepare the ORDER of that day to ensure that Kenig would never have to do any:

"HEAVY LIFTING"

TALK ABOUT DROPPING DONNELLY'S HAND

EXHIBIT 52 at LOT 1.com is Kenig's October 18, 2024 e-mail to Donnelly's Clerk:

Dear Judge Donnelly, attached is the proposed order in connection with the hearing this morning in the above matter.

EXHIBIT 53 at LOT 1.com is that October 18, 2024 ORDER as already prepared Kenig and then entered by Donnelly:

IT IS HEREBY ORDERED THAT:

1. **Defendant shall have until October 21, 2024 to file its appearance.**
2. **Defendant shall have until November 4, 2024 to answer or otherwise plead to the complaint**
3. **This matter is continued to November 19, 2024 at 9:00 a.m. for status of pleadings.**

"status of pleadings"

Kenig filed his mandatory APPEARANCE as the purported Attorney for Byline.

EXHIBIT 54 at LOT 1.com is the first Page of DEFENDANT'S 2-619 MOTION TO DISMISS PLAINTIFF'S COMPLAINT as filed on November 4, 2024:

Hearing Date: no hearing scheduled

At Page 11 of that MOTION:

As noted above, the Complaint alleges that Byline fraudulently foreclosed on the Properties by fraudulently fabricating a default under the loans based on the Barretts' failure to properly fund the real estate tax escrow at Byline. The Barretts made this identical argument in this Foreclosure Action which

was denied by Judge Robles and affirmed on appeal. Thus, res judicata applies because the final judgement on the matter was rendered by a court of competent jurisdiction which bars any subsequent actions between the same parties or their privies 011 the same cause of action.

"Properties"

Those are the identical criminal fraudulently fabricated physically impossible frauds upon the court of Kenig and then Robles and then Navarro and Mitchell and Mikva of:

The Sidwell map of Cook, attached hereto as Exhibit E, also shows that the two buildings are on separate, distinct lots. The commercial building sits on Lot "206" and the residential building sits on Lot "207".

For Kenig and then Robles and then Navarro and Mitchell and Mikva to fraudulently deny that PIN 206 was ever Class 2-12 to be assessed at 10% of market value but was always fraudulently fabricated **"misclassification"** of Class 517 to always by assessed at 25% of market value to fraudulently deny that it was Byline that had caused the criminal fraudulent foreclosure of the Barretts' actual continuous one Property:

AFTER

On October 23, 2018 Kenig had already admitted and verified that after the Barretts February 16, 2018 payment of $3,271.00 that the Barretts' actual real estate property tax account was already **"properly funded"**, with **SURPLUS**, to already both maintain Byline's REQUIRED LOW POINT BALANCE and to also already pay the actual 2nd installment property tax bill for Loan #11147585 due on August 1, 2018; there was never any PAST DUE AMOUNT of any amount under the actual provisions of Loan #11147585; the Barretts had paid Byline all of the monthly **"required"** payments under the actual provisions of LoN #11147585; the Barretts were never in any **"default"** of any nature under the actual provisions of their Loans with Byline; and it was Byline that had caused the criminal fraudulent foreclosure of the Barretts' actual continuous one Property; by criminally making it impossible for the Barretts to refinance their actual Loans with Byline elsewhere prior to maturity; with those two fraudulently fabricated **"default under the loans"** by the Barretts that never existed:

SURPLUS: $1,842.16

Escrow Balance (5,117.25)

Res judicata only applies to **"final"** decisions.

"Fraud upon the court" has been defined by the 7th Circuit Court of Appeals "to embrace that species of fraud which does, or attempts to, defile the court itself, or is fraud perpetrated by officers of the court so that the judicial machinery cannot perform in its usual manner its impartial task of adjudicating cases that are presented for adjudication." Kenner v. C.I.R., 387 F. 3d (1968) 7 Moore's Federal Practice. The 7th further stated a decision procured by fraud upon the court in essence a decision at all, and never becomes final.

None of the ORDERS and JUDGEMENTS as criminally entered by Robles and then Navarro and Mitchell and Mikva to criminally deny that it was Byline that had caused the criminal fraudulent foreclosure of the Barretts' actual continuous one Property were never in essence a decision at all and never became "final" for reason of the identical criminal fraudulently fabricated frauds upon the court of Kenig and Robles and Navarro and Mitchell and Mikva of fraudulently denying that actual genuine material criminal April 18, 2018 "demand letter" as prepared by Kenig ever existed; to criminally deny that it was Byline that had caused the criminal fraudulent foreclosure of the Barretts' actual continuous one Property:

APRIL 18, 2018 OCCURRED BEFORE MAY 8, 2018

CRIMEN OMNIA EX SE NATA VITIAT

OMNIA

On that November 19, 2024, Judge Donnelly and Kenig were already waiting for Frank Barrett with their already criminal conspiracy to defraud to dismiss the Barretts' COMPLAINT to criminally deny that it was Byline that had caused the criminal fraudulent foreclosure of the Barretts' actual continuous one Property.

When Frank Barrett approached the bench, he was informed by Judge Donnelly that Frank Barrett was there for a hearing on Byline's MOTION to dismiss the Barretts' COMPLAINT and only:

ORAL ARGUMENTS

Donnelly wanted only ORAL ARGUMENTS so Kenig did not have to do any:

HEAVY LIFTING

Frank Barrett objected and told Judge Donnelly that he was only in Donnelly's Courtroom that day for:

"status of pleadings"

Donnelly simply ignored Frank Barrett.

All Kenig had to say was:

"res judicata"

And Donnelly just simply granted Byline's Motion to dismiss the Barretts' COMPLAINT to fraudulently deny that it was Byline that had caused the criminal fraudulent foreclosure of the Barretts' actual continuous one Property.

EXHIBIT 55 at LOT 1.com is Kenig's November 19, 2024 e-mail to Donnelly's Clerk:

Christine, attached is draft of the proposed order in connection with the above matter that was up for hearing this morning.

"up for"

EXHIBIT 56 at LOT 1.com are the identical criminal frauds upon the court of Kenig and Donnelly as already prepared by Kenig and then criminally entered by Donnelly in the void November 19, 2024 ORDER:

This matter comes on the hearing on defendant's motion to dismiss plaintiff's complaint. Counsel for the defendant appearing via zoom and defendant Frank Barrett appearing in court prose, the Court having heard oral arguments and being advised,

There was never any criminally fabricated by Kenig and Donnelly **"hearing on defendant's motion to dismiss plaintiff's complaint"** ever **"up for"** on that November 19, 2024.

IT IS HEREBY ORDERED THAT the Court grants the defendant's 2-619 (a) (4) motion to dismiss plaintiff's complaint on the grounds of res ***judicata.***

res judicate only applies to **"final"** decisions.

NONE of the Orders and Judgements as criminally entered by Robles and then Navarro and Mitchell and Mikva and now Donnelly to criminally deny that it was Byline that had caused the criminal foreclosure of the Barretts' actual continuous one Property were never in essence any decision at all and never became **"final"** for reason of those criminal fraudulent fabricated frauds upon the court of Robles and then Navarro and Mitchell and Mikva and now Donnelly.

Exactly because of that criminal conspiracy to defraud of Kenig and now Donnelly to fraudulently deny that it was Byline that had caused the criminal fraudulent foreclosure of the Barretts' actual continuous one Property, on February 27, 2025 the Barretts filed a COMPLAINT FOR DAMAGES FOR FRAUDULENT FORECLOSURE AND OTHER RELIEF and SUMMONS with a mandatory court appearance of April 24, 2025; Case No. 2025L002772: Judge Patrick Sherlock Presiding: Calendar Q.

On April 21, 2025 Kenig filed his APPEARANCE as the purported Attorney for Byline and a ONE HUNDED AND SEVENTY-THREE PAGE Motion to have Case No. 2025L002772 be reassigned to Donnelly, for obvious reason.

Kenig really did not want Judge Sherlock to ever see the Barretts' COMPLAINT.

At that April 24, 2025 hearing, Judge Sherlock did not buy any of Kenig's obvious obfuscations; denied Kenig's Motion to have the Case reassigned to Donnelly and if Byline wanted that Case reassigned to Donnelly, then Kenig had to go to Judge Flannigan; and Judge Sherlock continued the matter to a May 28, 2025 status hearing.

EXHIBIT 57 at LOT 1.com is Kenig's April 25, 2025 NOTICE OF MOTION for a May 8, 2025 hearing on Kenig's motion to transfer Case No. 2025L002772 to

Donnely again with a ONE HUNDRED AND SEVENTY THREE page DEFENDANT'S MOTION TO REASSING CASE TO CALENDAR W: Donnelly: Judge Kathy Flanagan Presiding.

At that May 8, 2025 hearing, Frank Barrett objected to that Motion: OBVIOUSLY.

Judge Flanagan recognized Frank Barrett's objection but informed him that as a matter of administration procedure the Case had to be reassigned to Calander W: Donnelly.

Frank Barrett:

That's OK Judge Flanagan. Its all coming back anyway for follow the money.

FOLLOW THE MONEY; IT WAS ALWAYS THAT SIMPLE

For YEARS Kenig would just simply sit in his office and have fraudulent Order after fraudulent Order and fraudulent Judgement after fraudulent Judgement typed with criminal frauds upon the court to all criminally denying that it was Byline that had caused the criminal fraudulent foreclosure of the Barretts' actual continuous one Property.

For those YEARS , first Robles, and now Donnelly would just simply criminally enter WHATEVER fraudulent Order or fraudulent Judgement put in front of Robles and now Donnelly to fraudulently deny that it was Byline that had caused the criminal fraudulent foreclosure of the Barretts' actual continuous one Property and never had to worry for one second of criminally doing so because of the Cook County Appellate Court and the Illinois Supreme Court: **OBVIOUSLY.**

NOWHERE in the 3,934 Pages of that fraudulent Foreclosure Action was there a sample of Kenig's handwriting: **NOWWHERE:**

EXCEPT

That forever void June 19, 2019 ORDER APPOINTING RECEIVER FOR NON-RESEDENTIAL PROPERTY as criminally entered by clueless Robles on that June 19, 2019.

EXHIBIT 58 at LOT 1.com is the May 8, 2025 ORDER as already prepared by Kenig and then entered by Judge Flanagan over the objection of Frank Barrett:

WHERE HAVE WE SEEN THIS BEFORE

Paragraph 5. That is Kenig's **HANDWRITING**.

Paragraph 9a: No **THE COURT FINDS** ever comes with **FILL IN THE BLANK**.

Paragraph 12; 13; and 15: No **THE COURT FINDS** ever comes with **FILL IN THE BLANK**.

Those were never **THE COURT FINDS** of clueless Robles rendered AFTER that June 19, 2019 hearing as demanded by Byline for the fraudulent procurement of that Receiver.

Those were the criminally fabricated by Kenig physically impossible **THE COURT FINDS** as already prepared by Kenig on June 1, 2019.

What was criminally entered by clueless Robles on that June 19, 2019 were Kenig's fraudulently fabricated physically impossible criminal frauds upon the court of:

The Sidwell map of Cook County, attached hereto as Exhibit E, also shows that the two buildings are on separate, distinct lots. The commercial building sits on Lot "206" and **the residential building sits on Lot "207".**

If Judge Flanagan had not ruled against the Barretts for administrative reasons only, then the Barretts would never have had a sample of Kenig's:

HANDWRITING

APRIL 18, 2018 OCCURRED BEFORE MAY 8, 2018

CRIMEN OMNIA EX SE NATA VITIAT

OMNIA

Thank you, Judge Flanagan.

THE LORD DOES PROVIDE

To be continued ....

www.ingramcontent.com/pod-product-compliance
Lightning Source LLC
LaVergne TN
LVHW070856210926
848482LV00016B/951
* 9 7 9 8 3 4 9 4 9 8 9 9 2 *